THE
AVIATOR

THE AVIATOR

a screenplay by

John Logan

MIRAMAX BOOKS

NEW YORK

Copyright © 2004 John Logan

All rights reserved. No part of this book may be used or reproduced in any manner whatsoever without the written permission of the Publisher. Printed in the United States of America. For information address: Hyperion, 77 West 66th Street, New York, New York 10023-6298.

ISBN 1-4013-5970-1

FIRST EDITION

10 9 8 7 6 5 4 3 2 1

FOREWORD
by Leonardo DiCaprio

Mysterious, challenging, visionary, sinister, tormented. All words that apply to Howard Hughes. All facets of the character John Logan created in his script *The Aviator*. My job was to bring as much reality as I could to that complex character.

My relationship with Howard Hughes began about five years ago when I first started talking to John about the script. Over 15 drafts, I saw the story develop into something I felt was exciting: an historical movie that wasn't a dry recounting of facts but instead was an intense character study of a very troubled man. When my invaluable colleague and collaborator, the brilliant Martin Scorsese, agreed to direct the movie I felt we had an opportunity to create something special.

Marty, John and I spent a lot of time working together: going through the script, reading scenes aloud, acting them out, discussing options, debating dialogue, digging through mountains of historical research. We tried to investigate every aspect of the real Howard's life to discover the emotional and dramatic truth behind the character in the movie. We all wanted to create an honest and unsentimental picture of who this man really was, to celebrate his *complexity*. We wanted to present his sharp edges and disturbing phobias as much as his undeniable panache and daring. I know we are all proud of the results.

As an actor, one of the most challenging aspects of creating Howard Hughes was in exploring the psychological demons that tormented him throughout his life. (Nowadays he would be medically diagnosed as suffering from Obsessive Compulsive Disorder with a compounding germ phobia.) Since Howard's illness is such an important part of who he was, I felt it was vital that I treat it seriously and with respect. To gain a better understanding of what O.C.D. really is, I interviewed doctors and studied the behavior of actual patients. I wanted to make sure Howard's symptoms were accurate and honestly presented. This process allowed me a glimpse, at least, into the Hell that he often had to endure.

The culmination of all these efforts, coupled with John Logan's intricately developed screenplay, gave Martin Scorsese the chance to do what he does best—create unforgettable cinema.

The experience of working with both John and Marty truly gave me a deeper understanding of how challenging it is to condense a man's life into a screenplay. Particularly a man as multidimensional and utterly perplexing as Mr. Howard Hughes.

INTRODUCTION

by Martin Scorsese

September 22, 2004

When I started reading John Logan's script for *The Aviator*, I was immediately engrossed. I was fascinated by the drama of this young man, possessed by a vision of speed and flight and committing all of his resources to sharing that vision with the world.

And then, I realized that the young man happened to be Howard Hughes. This is rare—to take a real historical figure, almost a legendary one, and get the audience involved in the drama of his life from page one. In other words, John had written a wonderfully complex character, rather than a Famous Man, a story rather than a historical pageant.

I was intrigued by the idea of bringing Old Hollywood to life through Hughes' unique viewpoint. When he made *Hell's Angels* (a picture I've always loved), he was a truly independent filmmaker, and he literally spent years and a small fortune trying to get it right. I was intrigued by Hughes' adversarial relationship with Pan Am founder Juan Trippe, which resulted in a dramatic appearance before the Senate War Investigating Committee in 1947.

Most of all, though, I was intrigued by Hughes. I was born in 1942, so I was too young to have actually lived through the age of aviation, in which he was a true pioneer. I had only been aware of him as a talented eccentric recluse—the Hughes of legend. But John Logan had done something remarkable—he had given us the young Howard Hughes in all of his extraordinary complexity. He had seen not only the grandeur but the beauty of Hughes' life. He had written a character who was both tragic and triumphant, whose brilliance was inseparable from his mania, whose vulnerability was inseparable from his callousness, whose private vision of perfection drove him forward and stopped him dead in his tracks, and then drove him forward once more.

Which is to say that *The Aviator* was a portrait of an artist, writ large across the landscape of 20th century America.

Leonardo DiCaprio was the man who brought this project to my attention. His dedication to the role was absolutely remarkable. He dug deep, going way beyond the surface eccentricities and obsessive-compulsive behavior. He went all the way to the all-too-human core of this man called Howard Hughes. Honestly, I don't know how he did it, and the purity of his finished performance astonishes me.

I owe a debt to a brilliant cast, from Alec Baldwin as Trippe and Alan Alda as Senator Owen Brewster to John C. Reilly as Hughes' right hand man Noah Dietrich and the wonderful Cate Blanchett as Katherine Hepburn. And to my cinematographer, Bob Richardson; my production designer, Dante Ferretti; to Howard Shore, for a wonderful and often daring score; to my editor, Thelma Schoonmaker; and to a legion of people, behind the camera and in front of it, who helped me bring this wonderful project to the screen.

But the most significant contribution was from Howard Hughes, who lived a life as complex and extravagant, as tortured and obsessed, as rich and ultimately as mysterious as one can imagine.

THE AVIATOR

INT. VICTORIAN ROOM. NIGHT.

Out of darkness, hands . . .

Elegant hands, a woman's hands, a shimmering diamond ring catching the flickering gaslight. The hands dip into a large bowl of water. Wet now, the hands rise to meet naked flesh.

The **WOMAN** speaks, a too-genteel Southern lilt to her voice.

                    WOMAN
Q . . . U . . . A . . . R . . .

Her hands stroke the naked flesh before her, caressing and cleaning in equal measure. Her hands sensually move along arms, torso, legs . . .

                    WOMAN
. . . A . . . N . . . T . . .

The woman is kneeling before a standing **BOY**. He is naked. Nine years old. She is bathing him in the midst of an airless, ornate and darkly-paneled room. Oppressive silhouettes of late Victorian splendor in the shadows.

                    WOMAN
. . . I . . . N . . . E.

The naked **BOY** stands before her, used to the ritual.

                    BOY
Quarantine. Q . . . U . . . A . . . R . . .

The woman continues to bathe him, slowly stroking along his skin with her wet hands, the water trickling down his body. Unnaturally sensuous.

        BOY
 ...A...N...T...

She continues to bathe him, studying every inch of his skin, every pore, with her expressive hands. Her hands are microscopes.

        BOY
 ...I...N...E. Quarantine.

        WOMAN
You know the cholera? You've seen the signs on the houses where the coloreds live?

        BOY
Yes, mother.

        WOMAN
You know typhus?

        BOY
Yes, mother.

        WOMAN
You know what they can do to you?

        BOY
Yes, mother.

        WOMAN
You are not safe.

She continues to bathe him.

His expression is neutral. Calm

He is **HOWARD ROBARD HUGHES, JR.**

>   HOWARD (V.O.)
>   Don't tell me I can't do it . . . !

Taking us to . . .

EXT. AIR FIELD DAY

HOWARD HUGHES, a vital and energetic 21, is striding past the propeller of a vintage World War I biplane. And then another. And another.

>   HOWARD
>   . . . Don't tell me it can't be done!

Title: Hollywood, 1927.

He is walking with his STUNT COORDINATOR and DIRECTOR OF PHOTOGRAPHY.

>   STUNT COORDINATOR
>   The gyro forces are too much. You send the planes into simultaneous barrel-rolls and—

>   HOWARD
>   It's the damn climax of the picture, Frank. You make it work! Decrease the vertical trajectory if you have to. A LeRhone rotary won't stall at 60 degrees. I've done it.

>   DIRECTOR OF PHOTOGRPAHY
>   Howard, we're still short two cameras. We need to cut the sequence down to accommodate—

                            HOWARD
We're not cutting anything. I'll get the cameras. Set up for
rehearsal in five.

The **STUNT COORDINATOR** and **DIRECTOR OF PHOTOGRAPHY**
veer off to a team of waiting filmmakers as Howard continues striding past
the endless row of airplanes.

NOAH DIETRICH, 30s, catches up with **HOWARD**. **NOAH** is a
gruff-talking former real estate salesman and prizefighter. Currently a corporate accountant in desperate need of a corporation.

HOWARD's size strikes **NOAH** first. Six foot three. Rail-thin. And then
the looks. Dazzling. Movie star dazzling.

                            NOAH
Mr. Hughes, I'm Noah Dietrich, your office said—

                            HOWARD
Walk with me, Mr. Dietrich . . .

The voice. A bit louder than **NOAH** expected. Flat, a slight Texan twang.

                            HOWARD
You're a man on the come. Read your resume and talked to
your references. You know what I'm looking for?

                            NOAH
As I understand it you're looking for a second-in-command at
Hughes Tool—someone to help oversee the financial aspects of
the business—

                            HOWARD
I'm looking for someone to run it and do a damn good job.
There's really only one thing you gotta know: my folks are
gone now *so it's my money*. Now what I do with that money may

seem a bit crazy to those sonsofbitches in Houston—I'm sure it does—but it all makes good sense to me. You got that?

NOAH

Got it.

HOWARD

You made 5,200 dollars a year on your last job. I'll pay you 10,000.

NOAH

I guess I'll be working twice as hard.

HOWARD

You'll be working four times as hard. I just got you at half price. Welcome aboard, Mr. Dietrich.

Still walking, **HOWARD** shakes his hand. **NOAH** can't believe it.

HOWARD

You're my voice, make 'em understand that. Some of those fine folks down there still call me "Junior." You tell them it's "Mr. Hughes" now.

NOAH

You bet . . . So when do we go to Houston?

HOWARD

We're not. Choleria epidemic of 1913—two thousand dead. Whole place is nothing but a pestilential swamp. Typhus, malaria, cholera, yellow fever, you name it, they got it.

HOWARD has passed the last airplane. He stops, turns. He takes it in. Smiles.

And finally we see it all.

A vast sea of airplanes. His airplanes. It is staggering.

>   HOWARD
> You see that, Mr. Dietrich? You're looking at the largest private air force in the world . . . what do you think of that now?

A beat as **NOAH** takes in the world of airplanes.

>   NOAH
> It's your money.

HOWARD laughs and strides off toward the waiting film crew, waving his hand in a circle above his head.

>   HOWARD
> START 'EM UP!

And the airplanes roar to life as the propeller men send the props spinning.

Title: HELL'S ANGELS. Year One.

INT. AMBASSADOR HOTEL—COCOANUT GROVE NIGHTCLUB. NIGHT.

HOWARD enters the swirling heart of 1920's Hollywood nightlife. He is a scarecrow in a brown suit amidst a sea of tuxedos and silk.

A saucy vocalist croons the latest Gershwin Brothers' hit, "I'll Build a Stairway to Paradise," as **HOWARD** makes his way through the throngs, looking for someone.

>   VOCALIST
> "I"ll build a stairway to Paradise,
> With a new step every day . . ."

HOWARD spots MGM titan **LOUIS B. MAYER** standing at the bar with a few of his **CRONIES**. **HOWARD** goes to him:

> HOWARD
> Hello, Mr. Mayer, I don't know if you remember me, my name is Howard Hughes and I wanted to talk to you—

> MAYER
> The airplane picture.

HOWARD subtly turns his right ear towards **MAYER** so he can hear better, our first clue of **HOWARD**'s hearing impairment:

> HOWARD
> HELL'S ANGELS, right. Listen, I'm in a helluva bind and need your help. I want to rent some cameras.

Meanwhile, a man watches them closely from a table. He is **JOHNNY MEYER**, a jovial, fast-talking Hollywood press agent, fixer and pimp.

> MAYER
> *(amused)*
> All that oil money not enough to buy a few cameras?

> HOWARD
> Drill bits.

> MAYER
> Sorry?

> HOWARD
> My company makes drill bits. I already bought every camera I could but we're shooting our big dogfight scene this weekend and I need two more. You think MGM could help me out?

MAYER

MGM isn't usually in the practice of helping out the competition.

CRONY

How many cameras you have now?

HOWARD

Twenty-four.

MAYER'S CRONIES laugh.

MAYER

Jesus Christ! Look, Sonny—

HOWARD

Howard.

MAYER

Howard. Whoever you are. Here's my advice: you take your oil money and—

HOWARD

Drill . . . bits.

MAYER

You put it in the bank.

HOWARD

Sir, I need—

MAYER

Because if you continue making this picture you know what you'll have? A movie no one will distribute and no one wants to see and no more oil money. Welcome to Hollywood.

He smiles.

> HOWARD
> *(terse)*
> I'll be sure to remember that, Mr. Mayer.

MAYER turns back to his cronies, satisfied. **HOWARD** spots **JOHNNY MEYER** and goes to him:

> JOHNNY
> Hiya, boss.

> HOWARD
> *(shaking hands)*
> Johnny.

A beautiful **WAITRESS** glides up as **JOHNNY** lights a cigarette.

> JOHNNY
> Whiskey and soda but not too much soda. Hell, nix the soda.

> HOWARD
> Milk, please. In a bottle with the cap still on.

She glides off.

> JOHNNY
> Okay, Howard, what'd he say?

> HOWARD
> Sonofabitch won't part with a single goddamn camera.

> JOHNNY
> So make do with what you have.

HOWARD
What I have isn't enough, not for how I see it . . .

As **HOWARD** speaks he quietly reaches across the table and takes **JOHNNY**'s cigarette, stubs it out in the ashtray. He is not even aware he is doing it. **JOHNNY** is too smart to protest. Howard then cleans the table in front of him with a napkin.

HOWARD
. . . My *name* depends on this picture. If it doesn't work, I'm back to Houston with my tail between my legs, making goddamn drill bits for the rest of my life.

JOHNNY
Couldn't you find a way to do it with the cameras you have? Just be creative.

HOWARD
Johnny, you're a press agent, you're supposed to know all the little ins and outs of Hollywood. Do you?

JOHNNY
Absolutely.

HOWARD
Good. Leave the *big ideas* to me.

He casually drops the now-soiled napkin on the floor as a beautiful **CIGARETTE GIRL** comes to the table, she leans forward, offering her wares:

CIGARETTE GIRL
Cigar, Cigarette, Sen-Sen?

HOWARD is instantly focused on her, the rest of the world does not exist.

HOWARD
I don't smoke—but you could help me with something else.

                    CIGARETTE GIRL
Yeah?

                         HOWARD
You could show me what gives a beautiful woman like you
pleasure.

JOHNNY almost chokes. The CIGARETTE GIRL looks at **HOWARD**.

                         HOWARD
Say you're just standing there and I touch you . . . Just with
my fingertips . . . Would you like that? . . . I want to learn
what pleases you. I want to learn *everything* about you . . . Will
you let me do that?

She looks at him.

                    CIGARETTE GIRL
I'm off in half an hour.

                         HOWARD
I'm in room 217.

She goes.

                         HOWARD
(standing)
Johnny, get on the horn to Universal and Warners. I need two
more cameras by Saturday. Rent 'em if you can. Steal 'em if
you have to.

He goes. **JOHNNY** watches him cut through the crowd, dumbstruck.

INT. AIR FIELD—COMMAND TENT. NIGHT.

A makeshift screening room.

HOWARD sits, slumped in a chair, watching dailies from HELL'S ANGELS. A handful of pilots and filmmakers sit around the tent as well.

They are watching some footage from the climactic dogfight sequence, planes soaring through the air. But the footage is curiously impotent, lacking excitement.

HOWARD, sinking deeper into his chair, watches the planes zooming about on the screen.

> HOWARD
> Goddamn! . . . Why the hell does it look so slow? This isn't what it was like up there . . . They look like a bunch of goddamn models!

HOWARD stands and walks to the screen, a growing realization.

> HOWARD
> Jesus Christ . . .

> STUNT COORDINATOR
> Howard?

HOWARD stands at the screen. The flickering images of the planes wash over him as he explains:

> HOWARD
> Without something *standing still* behind the planes we got no idea how fast we're moving. We got no idea of *relative motion!* . . . *(he spins to an aide)* . . . Call over to UCLA. Get me the best meteorologist they got. Get him here in an hour.

He strides out of the Command Tent.

EXT. AIR FIELD. NIGHT.

HOWARD lopes, discontent, away from the Command Tent toward an illuminated area of the field.

HOWARD's personal plane—a nifty Boeing Scout biplane—is at the center of a hive of activity. A team of his engineers are working on the plane.

GLENN ODEKIRK sees HOWARD approaching and goes to him. GLENN is a brilliant engineer with an innovative imagination. He is one of the few people HOWARD sees as his friend, not as an employee.

GLENN
Hey, you want the good news or the bad news?

HOWARD
Bad news, always.

They move to the plane, considering the engine in particular:

GLENN
We installed the 450 radial—but the struts won't take the vibration. Minute we go contact the struts start cracking at the attach points.

HOWARD
What's the good news?

GLENN
There isn't any.

HOWARD
Dammit, Odie, if the 450's too big figure something else out!

HOWARD circles the plane like a predator, GLENN following:

GLENN

We've done everything—we've rebuilt her from top to bottom. If we drain the fuel tank for a couple of runs she might make 180 mph.

HOWARD

I want minimum 200.

GLENN

Yeah, well I want a date with Theda Bara but that ain't gonna happen either.

HOWARD

Don't be so sure . . . Okay, okay, okay—This is a simple engineering problem. We just gotta think it out . . .

HOWARD carefully examines the plane, taking special note of the struts connecting the upper and lower wings. As:

HOWARD

So if the struts won't sustain the engine we need—then we gotta get rid of the struts.

GLENN

Then the top wing falls off.

HOWARD stands back, considering the plane. His mind racing.

HOWARD

Then let it.

GLENN

What?

HOWARD

Who says we need a top wing?

GLENN looks at him. Curious.

                    HOWARD

Who says we need anything?

GLENN approaches, savoring the idea in his mind, excited by **HOWARD**'s bold vision.

                    GLENN

A monoplane . . .

                    HOWARD

A cantilevered monoplane. They're doing it in France. To hell with the top wing and the struts—

                    GLENN

550 Whitney Wasp engine—

                    HOWARD

100 octane fuel will give us a top horsepower of—what?

                    GLENN

700.

                    HOWARD

Squeeze it to a thousand and we got the fastest plane ever built.

They look at each other. Smiling.

Out of such moments are magnificent creatures born.

                    GLENN

You know, I just gotta say . . . we've already spent over 200,000 dollars rebuilding this plane.

                    HOWARD
To hell with it . . . *(he smiles)* . . . Tear it up, Odie.

He strides off into the darkness.

GLENN watches him go.

Then he picks up a sledgehammer. His engineers watch, horrified.

GLENN swings the sledgehammer—CRASH—and annihilates the struts on one side of the plane. The top wing immediately snaps in two and falls.

INT. COMMAND TENT—AIRFIELD. NIGHT.

A bookish and bespectacled man sits nervously. His hair shows all the rumpled signs of a man roused from sleep.

He is **PROFESSOR FITZ**, a meteorologist. **HOWARD** is with him.

                 PROFESSOR FITZ
Well . . . the, um, cumulonimbus formations you speak of that look like . . .

                    HOWARD
Giant breasts full of milk. I want clouds, dammit.

                 PROFESSOR FITZ
Yes, clouds that look like, um, giant breasts full of milk cannot be exactly guaranteed for any particular location. You might have to . . . um . . . wait.

                    HOWARD
Then we'll wait . . . *(he stands, preparing to go)* . . . Whatever they pay you at UCLA, I'm doubling it. You work for me now. Find some clouds.

He begins to go. Immediately stops and returns. Repeating the exact same words and gestures:

> HOWARD
> You work for me now. Find some clouds.

He strides out of the tent, completely unaware of the peculiar repetition.

We hear his voice from outside the tent:

> HOWARD (V.O.)
> Find some clouds!

A **PILOT** lounging in the command tent turns to **FITZ**.

> PILOT
> Welcome to HELL'S ANGELS.

EXT. AIR FIELD-FRONT GATE. DAY.

NOAH drives up to the air field. A sign hangs on the front gate: "WAR POSTPONED. NO CLOUDS."

He glances at the sign and drives onto the field.

EXT. AIR FIELD. DAY.

HOWARD is slowly moving around an early prototype of what will become his astounding H-1 Racer plane. He feels along the aerodynamic sides and engine cowling. His sensitive fingertips take in every inch of the plane like a lover.

GLENN ODEKIRK is working with his team of engineers and mechanics.

Everywhere else around the air field, idleness. The planes wait. The pilots and mechanics play cards.

The sky is cloudless.

Title: HELL'S ANGELS. Year Two.

PROFESSOR FITZ is following **HOWARD** as he moves around the plane. Poor **PROFESSOR FITZ** is going mad. His hair flies out wildly in all directions. It is, needless to say, the only thing flying.

                    HOWARD
... We've been to Chatsworth, Santa Cruz, Encino, San Diego, Riverside, Van Nuys and Bakersfield. It's been eight months! *Where are the goddamn clouds?!*

                    PROFESSOR FITZ
(cracking up)
They move, Mr. Hughes! Clouds move! That's what they do! They moooove!

                    HOWARD
It's costing me 5,271 dollars *a day* keeping these planes on the ground. You find me some goddamn clouds!

PROFESSOR FITZ scurries off as **NOAH** drives up. **NOAH** climbs out of his car and goes to **HOWARD**. **HOWARD** continues to carefully feel along the plane.

                    NOAH
Nice day.

                    HOWARD
Very funny.

                    NOAH
I got a call from Houston. They're getting real nervous about all of this.

HOWARD
Then stop showing them the damn bills.

NOAH
That's illegal, Howard.

HOWARD
Shit no, maybe it's a little naughty.

NOAH
Hughes Tool is incorporated in Texas, they have to see the bills.

HOWARD dips under the new cowling over the engine, feeling the rivets connecting it to the plane:

HOWARD
Then incorporate a new division out here. Call it Hughes Aircraft . . . (to **GLENN**) . . . Odie, do we need these rivets on the cowling?

GLENN
Yeah, or the reverse thrust would rip it off.

HOWARD
They're gonna give me drag. Do something about that okay?

GLENN
Wind resistance on the *rivets?*

HOWARD
I want her slippery.

HOWARD stalks away, **NOAH** following.

NOAH
Howard, there are serious tax consequences to incorporating in California—

HOWARD
Just take care of it, would ya?

PROFESSOR FITZ comes running up to **HOWARD**, bursting, waving weather charts.

PROFESSOR FITZ
Oakland! Clouds in Oakland!

HOWARD
You mean it this time?

PROFESSOR FITZ
YES! GODDAMN IT, YES! I PROMISE YOU CLOUDS IN OAKLAND!

HOWARD looks at him, amused.

HOWARD
No need to get all jittery now.

HOWARD turns to the aviators:

HOWARD
OAKLAND! WE'RE GOING TO OAKLAND!

The air field springs to life, pilots running flat out for their planes.

NOAH watches it all. Madness.

EXT. OAKLAND AIRFIELD. DAY.

Clouds, glorious clouds. Cumulonimbus clouds like giant breasts bursting with milk.

Imagine, if you can, forty planes filling the same air space. Stick your head in a hornet's nest and you might have some idea.

This is the climactic battle of HELL'S ANGELS in the making.

The planes twist and spin, arcing through the clouds, the clouds giving a scale to the action. The planes zoom back and forth recklessly, shooting into view and then disappearing again, exponentially increasing until the sky is an impossible jumble of planes. Forty engines roar as forty pilots try to avoid collision.

It is mayhem. It is poetry.

And in the midst of it all . . .

INT./EXT. CAMERA PLANE FOLLOWING.

. . . is **HOWARD**.

He is in the camera plane, directing the action. He squawks into a handheld microphone—radio control to the air field and to the other planes—and flings instructions, pointing madly in various directions. All words are lost in the howl of the many engines. A cameraman cranks beside him.

Two planes zoom past—almost clipping the camera plane—**HOWARD** doesn't care.

We are inside the hornet's nest now. A beautiful order emerging from the chaos as the planes dogfight.

Our spirits soar with **HOWARD**. It is totally exhilarating.

INT. HOLLYWOOD NIGHTCLUB. NIGHT.

A great ice sculpture of a biplane and the words "HELL'S ANGELS" loom over a banquet table.

The HELL'S ANGELS wrap party. **JOHNNY MEYER** is gossiping with a starlet. **GLENN ODEKIRK** is drinking with his engineers. **PROFESSOR FITZ** and aviators and actors and filmmakers celebrate the long-awaited completion of the movie.

HOWARD stands a bit away from the festivities, watching, thinking. Noah stands talking to him.

HOWARD'S POV—EXTREME CLOSEUP—**NOAH** talking—his lips jabbering out muffled words—

It is extremely startling. **NOAH**'s voice is strangely dim, echoing through a tunnel of insistent, droning white noise. We realize the depth of **HOWARD**'s deafness.

Finally, **HOWARD** subtly turns his good right ear to **NOAH** and forces himself to concentrate:

>   NOAH
> . . . I mean you have to admit it . . . Now honestly, did you actually think you'd ever finish the damn thing?

>   HOWARD
> *(smiles)*
> Come with me.

INT. MOVIE THEATER. NIGHT.

AL JOLSON is on the screen. Singing. THE JAZZ SINGER.

HOWARD and **NOAH** stand at the back of the theater.

>   HOWARD
> You see, this is what people want. Silent pictures are yester-

day's news, so I figure I have to reshoot HELL'S ANGELS for sound.

                    NOAH

How much of it?

                    HOWARD

All of it.

NOAH stares at him, speechless.

                    HOWARD

Before you even ask, I'll tell you: an additional 1.7 million. We got that much?

                    NOAH

No!

                    HOWARD

Well, then we better make it. Take care of that, would ya? . . . *(he watches the screen, delighted)* . . . Sound, Noah, sound!

EXT. 7000 ROMAINE. NIGHT.

7000 Romaine Street, in the heart of Hollywood, is a rather attractive Art Deco building. The walls are yellow stucco.

There is no sign to indicate this modest building is the home to **HOWARD**'s many enterprises.

INT. 7000 ROMAINE—HALLWAY. NIGHT.

It may be midnight, but the joint is jumping. Business never stops for Hughes Tool, Hughes Aircraft and HELL'S ANGELS.

Secretaries swirl around desks and in and out of offices, they have to slither past the huge editing machines set up in the hallways. Twelve editors and their many assistants are laboring over Movieolas, stitching together the film. They are toiling with, believe it or not, 500 hours of film.

The whole building is a jungle of celluloid, the spools and film strips hanging down like vines.

Title: HELL'S ANGELS. Year Three.

INT. 7000 ROMAINE—SCREENING ROOM. NIGHT.

HOWARD's church.

His retreat from the world. His peaceful oasis from everything and everyone, if such a thing were possible.

The screening room is large and well-appointed. Thick red velvet seats and a large screen, currently showing some dogfight footage.

We see **HOWARD** from behind. He is slumped in a chair, long legs stretched out on the seat ahead of him. Shoes off. Sipping a bottle of milk. The light from the projector flickering over his head.

We revolve around him. See his face. And are surprised.

He is unshaven. Exhausted. His eyes red.

A red light blinks over the doors to the room.

                    HOWARD.
Who is it?

                    NOAH (V.O.)
Noah.

                    HOWARD
Come in.

NOAH enters.

NOAH
I've been on the phone to Houston for three solid hours now— we've been fixing every goddamn book we have but—

HOWARD
Wait.

He watches the screen. Dogfighting footage. He picks up a phone to the projection booth:

HOWARD (ON PHONE)
Run reel ten. I think we're duplicating a shot . . . And tell Jimmy I'd like ten chocolate chip cookies. Medium chips, none too close to the outside. Thanks . . . (hangs up, continues to **NOAH**) . . . Do you remember this shot from reel ten?

NOAH
No, I don't remember anything from reel ten. I don't know what reel ten is. I'm a businessman, Howard. So are you . . .

He sits. He speaks very seriously. Very gently.

NOAH
This has been a great ride and we've had a hell of a lot of fun . . . But you're losing 25,000 dollars a day doing this. Every day.

HOWARD
What are my options?

NOAH
I don't know that you have any. I'm afraid you gotta close it down and dig your way out . . . I'm sorry, Howard. I truly am.

A long beat as **HOWARD**'s movie flickers. He watches it, his dream.

Then the flickering stops. The dream gone. Darkness. The only sound is **HOWARD**'s heavy breathing.

PROJECTIONIST (V.O.)
Reel ten, Mr. Hughes.

Another reel starts up. Flickering light. More dogfighting action.

HOWARD
Mortgage Toolco. Every asset.

NOAH looks at him. Prays he hasn't heard correctly.

HOWARD
You heard me.

NOAH
If you do that you could lose everything.

HOWARD
I won't.

A beat.

NOAH
All right. I'll get into it.

HOWARD
Thanks.

NOAH rises, leaves the room with the gait of a sleepwalker.

HOWARD sits, watching the movie.

Then he feels something on the arm of his chair.

Grease? Dirt? Dust? Imaginary? Real?

He looks at the arm of his chair:

HOWARD's POV—EXTREME CLOSEUP—the texture of the fabric of the arm of the chair.

He slowly raises his hands and holds them up like a surgeon after scrubbing. A disquieting image.

Then we hear the sound of a roaring crowd, taking us to . . .

EXT. HOLLYWOOD BOULEVARD. EVENING.

. . . The crowd roar is deafening. It is the biggest night in Hollywood. Ever.

The opening of HELL'S ANGELS.

An endless series of limousines slowly crawl up to the overwrought splendor of Grauman's Chinese, dispensing the elite to a blood red carpet. Masses of people fill the sidewalks. Savage klieg lights stab to the heavens.

We take in the barely controlled hysteria as we hear a **RADIO ANNOUNCER**:

> RADIO ANNOUNCER (V.O.)
> . . . More than a half a million good souls lining the curb of Hollywood Boulevard. Everyone is here tonight for the unveiling of HELL'S ANGELS, Howard Hughes' four million dollar epic. You heard me right, ladies and gentlemen, four million smackeroos . . .

We sweep down to find the **RADIO ANNOUNCER** coiled like a cobra behind a standing microphone on the red carpet, narrating the action.

We can see **JOHNNY MEYER** on the red carpet as well, directing traffic patterns into the theater and glad-handing.

                    RADIO ANNOUNCER
    . . . It is . . . The Most Expensive Movie Ever Made! Nothing
    five-and-dime for our Mr. Hughes . . . *(he sees* **JOHNNY
    MEYER** *waving at him)* . . . And now, ladies and gentlemen,
    I think—Yes, yes—I can just see Mr. Hughes' car arriving
    now . . .

HOWARD's limo pulls up, he emerges with **JEAN HARLOW**, the beautiful movie starlet.

He is utterly unprepared for the enormity of the response—

Blinding camera flashes—the flashbulbs instantly ejected and replaced—the shouted questions from reporters—the harsh phosphorous glare of the klieg lights—the great mob surging forward like a river dangerously close to cresting its banks.

The fans not only cheer and shout now, they scream.

A few desperate hands clutch forward through the throngs, past the rows of security guards, trying to touch, to feel, to be.

Howard sees the grasping hands.

HOWARD'S POV—EXTREME CLOSEUP—the grasping hands, the dirty nails—the filth—the screaming, gaping mouths of the fans-

Jean Harlow plays to the cameras with efficient grace.

                    RADIO ANNOUNCER
    . . . Mr. Hughes escorts the lovely starlet Jean Harlow tonight.
    He discovered her for this picture and we think her platinum
    blonde locks and Hot-Jazz-Babydoll style are gonna make her
    a big star . . . *(he beckons to them)* . . . Mr. Hughes! How 'bout a
    word?

HOWARD escorts JEAN toward the RADIO ANNOUNCER. He is shocked to find that they are treading over a sea of ejected flashbulbs. The flashbulbs crunch under their feet as they move down the red carpet.

They arrive at the RADIO ANNOUNCER:

>   RADIO ANNOUNCER
> Big night for you Mr. Hughes!

HOWARD can't hear over the screaming crowd.

>   RADIO ANOUNCER
>   (*a little louder*)
> Big night for you tonight!

>   HOWARD
> Very big.

>   RADIO ANNOUNCER
> Tell us what it was like making this fabulous picture.

HOWARD either didn't hear or chooses not to respond.

>   HOWARD
> Yes.

>   RADIO ANNOUNCER
> Yeah, um—So, four million clams from your own pocket, nervous how the flick will fly?

>   HOWARD
> Big night . . . Enjoy the show.

He leads JEAN into the theater.

INT. GRAUMAN'S CHINESE. NIGHT.

Needless to say, the unwashed masses aren't inside. The huge auditorium is crowded with tuxedos and gowns.

HELL'S ANGELS plays on a massive screen. The crowd loves it, oohing and aahing at the aerial pyrotechnics on the screen.

HOWARD sits, nervous, with JEAN. Clutching her hand.

HELL'S ANGELS ends. HOWARD slowly exhales.

The applause begins . . . builds . . . a cascading wave of applause. The audience stands. They face HOWARD. Applauding.

HOWARD sees NOAH standing, applauding with a look of unbelievable relief. HOWARD smiles.

> JEAN
> Stand up, Slim, take a bow.

HOWARD finally stands and waves a bit shyly. The crowd cheers for him.

INT. GRAUMAN'S CHINESE. LATER.

HOWARD strides with JEAN through the lobby, toward the doors out. A few AIDES are following, scribbling in pads.

> HOWARD
> . . . And reel four played way too long. Too many coughs. Get Harry and the team out of the party and get them over to the office—I want to cut a few shots tonight—And find Glenn Odekirk. Somebody write this down: flush rivets. You got that? Flush rivets.

                              AIDE
(scribbling in pad)
"Flush rivets."

HOWARD sweeps through the doors and out of the lobby to—

EXT. GRAUMAN'S CHINESE. NIGHT.

HOWARD strides from the theater and is met with half a million screams. Half a million cheers. The flashbulbs assault. The klieg lights swing in.

He is a butterfly pinned to a wall. He is on top of the world.

Even **JEAN** is shocked at the response. She hesitates. **HOWARD** does not. He walks forward down the red carpet and stops.

He stands, looks around at the sea of faces. The women. The promise.

The thin young man from Houston, all of 24 years old, has arrived.

EXT. BEACH. DAY.

A movie crew is on a lunch break.

Then a whine from above . . . growing into a roar from beyond the clouds . . .

A large Sikorsky Amphibian seaplane sweeps through the clouds. It is a dramatic if rather ungainly beast, all wing and convex hull. The Sikorsky makes a perfect landing. Splashing and thundering to a stop.

The movie people watch, speechless, as **HOWARD** climbs from the Sikorsky like Apollo from his chariot. He strides across the beach.

He approaches a tall, lean **WOMAN** lounging on a deck chair under an umbrella, her long legs stretched out. She wears pants.

He stops before her.

> HOWARD
> I read in the magazines that you play golf.

The woman looks up at him.

> WOMAN
> On occasion.

> HOWARD
> How about nine holes?

A beat as she considers him.

> WOMAN
> Now, Mr. Hughes?

> HOWARD
> If it would be convenient, Miss Hepburn.

And **KATHARINE HEPBURN** smiles.

EXT. GOLF COURSE. DAY.

The golf ball sails straight down the fairway. It doesn't slice. It doesn't hook. It wouldn't dare. It's perfect.

KATE HEPBURN insists on perfection.

There is a crisp, lean strength to **KATE**. She holds herself back. She controls. She is also exceedingly verbal, words pouring out of her in stream-of-consciousness flashes. She is maddening. She is magnificent.

HOWARD watches her ball sail over the fairway and land. Perfectly.

He lines up his shot. Swings. Very nice. But not perfect.

> KATE
> You're not extending enough on your follow through . . .

She speaks very quickly. And as if her perfect teeth are perpetually clenched together. Perhaps they open a few millimeters to allow her to eat.

She briskly takes off after her ball. He follows.

> KATE
> Follow through is everything in golf. Just like life, don't you find?—*(she laughs for a millisecond)*—Saw your SCARFACE picture. Violent.

> HOWARD
> Realistic.

> KATE
> Movies are movies, Howard, not life. Now the *stage* is real. Real flesh-and-blood human beings right there in front of you, buster. Can't look away. Can't munch popcorn. That would be rude. You like the theater?

> HOWARD
> No.

> KATE
> I adore the theater. Only alive on stage. I'll teach you. We'll see some Ibsen. If the *Republicans* haven't outlawed him by now. You're not a Republican, are you? Couldn't abide that. How did you vote in '32?

HOWARD
I didn't.

KATE
You must! It's your Sacred Franchise!

She arrives at her ball. Lines up. Another perfect shot. Her ball bounces to the green.

He lines up. Another good shot that also bounces to the green.

She strides along. He follows.

KATE
Heard you were wooing Ginger Rogers. What about that?

HOWARD
She's a friend.

KATE
Men can't be *friends* with women, Howard. They must possess them or leave them be. It's a primitive urge from the cave man days. It's all in Darwin. Hunt the flesh, kill the flesh, eat the flesh. That's the male sex all over.

HOWARD
(can't hear)
Excuse me?

KATE
Well, if you're deaf you must own up to it. Get a hearing aid. Or see my father. He's a urologist but it's all tied up inside the body, don't you find? I keep healthy. I take seven showers a day to keep clean. Also because I am what is so vulgarly referred to as "outdoorsy."

They move to the green.

                              KATE

   I'm not "outdoorsy." I'm athletic. I sweat. There it is. Now we
   both know the sordid truth. I sweat and you're deaf. Aren't we
   a fine pair of misfits?

She lines up and putts. Perfectly. The ball rolls into the hole.

                              KATE

   Three.

HOWARD lines up. Putts. Misses the hole by an inch.

                              KATE
   (delighted)
   Noble effort.

He taps the putt in.

                              KATE

   So I suppose you're wooing me now. Ah well.

She strides off to the next hole.

INT. H-1 AIRPLANE HANGAR. DAY.

HOWARD's hand . . . his fingertips . . . slowly moving across a plain of shining metal.

We see him reflected in the aluminum skin of the H-1, his amazing new racer plane. He runs his hand along the entire fuselage of the almost complete plane. **GLENN** and his team of engineers and mechanics wait nervously, watching **HOWARD**'s hand.

HOWARD continues to move along the fuselage, his fingertips feeling the plane. Sensual. Then his fingertips undulate over a line of rivets on the fuselage. He doesn't like that.

JACK FRYE follows HOWARD as he inspects the plane.

JACK, 30's, is a landmark figure in commercial aviation. He is a former WWI ace and barnstormer. His sweet, round face disguises his passionate commitment to his cause. For he is also . . .

Title: Jack Frye: President of TWA Airlines.

JACK
. . . now we got a fleet of DC-3's. But they're completely underpowered for our routes. We got the long routes straight across the damn country, right? So I figure we gotta get into the design racket.

HOWARD completes his inspection, turns to GLENN and his engineers:

HOWARD
Not enough . . . *(the engineers wilt)* . . . The rivets have to be completely flush, every screw and joint countersunk. No wind resistance on the fuselage. She's gotta be clean, Odie.

GLENN returns to his engineers as JACK continues to HOWARD:

JACK
So anyway, we're looking to build a new plane. A modern plane.

HOWARD
What kinda plane?

JACK
Okay. The DC-3's a dinosaur, too goddamn small. It has a ceiling of 7000 feet—

HOWARD
Something bigger.

JACK
Try 50 seats. With a ceiling of *12,000* feet.

HOWARD
No. 20,000 . . . (**JACK** *looks at him, stunned*) . . . What does 20,000 feet give you?

JACK
Less turbulence.

HOWARD
Right. 'Cause it's above the weather . . . We want to fly *above the weather.*

JACK
Jesus . . .

HOWARD
Only *one percent* of the American population has ever set foot on a commercial airliner. Why? Because they're scared to death. And they should be. 7,000 feet is bumpy as shit . . . We build a plane that flies *above* the weather and we could get every man, woman and child in this country to feel *safe* up there . . . An airplane with the ability to fly into the sub-stratosphere—across the country—across the world . . . Now that is the future.

JACK is transfixed by **HOWARD**'s bold vision.

HOWARD
Shoot straight with me now, I don't want to get into all this if your board doesn't have the balls for it. Will they support us?

JACK
I don't know. They're tight bastards.

                        HOWARD
What's your financial picture?

                         JACK
Not great.

                        HOWARD
Last year's deficit?

                         JACK
770,000.

                        HOWARD
What's it selling at?

                         JACK
Around eight dollars a share.

HOWARD considers.

                        HOWARD
Lowest it's been . . . I can do that.

                         JACK
Do what?

                        HOWARD
Buy it.

JACK stares at him.

                         JACK
You wanna buy the airline?

                        HOWARD
Sure, don't want a bunch of damn pencil-pushers getting

in the way of us building our plane. Gimme brass tacks now. What does controlling interest in TWA cost me?

JACK

Call it 15 million.

HOWARD whistles.

HOWARD

That's a chunk of change... *(checks his watch)*... Listen I gotta date. Call Noah Dietrich and have him start buying.

HOWARD begins to stride off...

JACK

Howard—hold on—are you sure? You wanna think about it for five minutes?

HOWARD

(calling back)
Hell, Jack, I got a tiger by the tail here, can't let it go.

He leaves the hangar. **JACK** watches him go, dumbstruck.

And **HOWARD** is on his way toward owning an airline.

INT. COCOANUT GROVE NIGHTCLUB. NIGHT.

An explosion of 1930's glamour.

A sea of tuxedos and shimmering dresses. The orchestra bounces something with a rolling swing edge. Dancers float around the dance floor in imperfect imitations of Fred and Ginger.

The MAITRE D' leads **HOWARD** and **KATE** to a table:

MAITRE D'
How goes the "aviation," Mr. Hughes?

HOWARD
Just fine, Pete.

MAITRE D'
I'm so glad.

He presents their table with a flourish, effortlessly pulling out **KATE**'s chair and snapping his fingers to their **WAITER** simultaneously. The Maitre D' disappears and their WAITER instantly appears in his place.

WAITER
Good evening, Mr. Hughes, Madame... The usual, Mr. Hughes?

HOWARD
Please.

WAITER
And may I recommend for the lady our clementine soup followed by roast wild duck with currant glaze and poached pears in rose sauce, it's truly divine.

KATE
Ah—that sounds fine.

The **WAITER** smiles and then crisply disappears. **KATE**, used to her fair share of attention, is actually speechless at the attention being paid to **HOWARD**.

He smiles, almost embarrassed.

KATE
Your kind of joint, is it? Wouldn't have thought.

HOWARD

They're open late. I go to a hot dog stand on La Cienega too. They're open until four.

KATE

Are they? How grand.

A familiar face bobs through the crowd toward them: **JOHNNY MEYER**. A rather liquid **ERROL FLYNN** with him.

JOHNNY

Howard! Sonofagun!

They join **KATE** and **HOWARD**. **ERROL**, every inch the dashing movie star, sloshes in next to **KATE**. She heartily disapproves of them both.

HOWARD

Kate, this is Johnny Meyer, sorta my press agent.

JOHNNY

Please-ta-meet-ya-loved-ya-in-ALICE-ADAMS.

KATE

You're too kind.

HOWARD

And you know Errol, I'm sure.

ERROL

(kisses her hand)
Kate, Kate, Kate of the Clench-Jawed Hepburns. Enchanting as always. You should use Lux on your hands, by the way, I do.

JOHNNY

Kate . . . *(she is offended by his chummy familiarity)* . . . You and Howard ought to cook up a picture. Costar with Errol. I could sell that in spades.

KATE

Oh, I think not. Don't you read VARIETY, Mr. Meyer? I'm "Box Office Poison." I'm on the outs, the skids, the doldrums, day-old fish not worth the eating, so they tell me.

ERROL

Hell with 'em. Soulless pricks to a man . . . (he sloshes his gaze to **HOWARD**) . . . Johnny tells me you're thinking about doing a Western, of all goddamn things.

HOWARD

Yeah, gonna call it THE OUTLAW—

JOHNNY

(to Kate)
And you know what it's about? S-E-X! It's all about S-E-X!

HOWARD

It's a *Western*.

ERROL

(to Howard)
You can't have *fornication* in a Western. Isn't done, old boy.

The **WAITER** appears with their food.

WAITER

Clementine soup for the lady . . . (presents **HOWARD**'s spartan meal with a flourish) . . . New York cut steak, twelve peas, bottle of milk with the cap on.

The **WAITER** goes. **HOWARD** carefully removes the cap from his milk as:

ERROL

Now Howard, if you're talking about finally putting carnality on the silver screen, you must swear to let me sit in on the casting sessions . . .

As **ERROL** speaks he casually reaches to **HOWARD**'s plate and picks up a pea. Tosses it into his mouth.

HOWARD freezes, stares at his plate. **KATE** notices.

HOWARD'S POV—EXTREME CLOSEUP—his plate—the peas. All sound drops to a sense of his muffled deafness. To **HOWARD** there is something horrible about his plate now. It has been infected by **ERROL**'s touch.

He stares at the plate, disturbed, as **ERROL** rattles on:

> ERROL (O.S.)
> . . . I'm somewhat know for my eye. My eye for "talent," isn't that right, Johnny?

> JOHNNY (O.S.)
> You oughta give up that prancing in tights and be a talent scout.

> ERROL (O.S.)
> That prancing in tights paid for my new yacht. You must all come sailing with me. Catalina this weekend, what do you say? I've even managed to coax the luscious Miss de Havilland and her equally luscious sister to accompany me—though I fear their not-remotely luscious mother will insist on coming along to protect their questionable "virtue." Ah well, we shall assault those twin monuments of pristine Britannic beauty nonetheless . . .

HOWARD tears himself back to reality:

> HOWARD
> I have to go . . . *(he stands, offers his hand to* **KATE***)* . . . If you'll excuse me, we have to be somewhere.

                    ERROL
You are somewhere, Howard.

                    HOWARD
Somewhere else.

KATE takes his hand and rises.

                    KATE
Charmed, gentlemen. Do help yourself to the poached pears, I hear they're divine.

ERROL and **JOHNNY** are a little mystified as **HOWARD** leads her away.

HOWARD and **KATE** cut through the crowd:

                    KATE
My hero . . . God, all that Hollywood talk bores me silly. As if there aren't more important things in the world! Mussolini, for one. Where are we going, by the way?

                    HOWARD
Feel like a little adventure?

                    KATE
Do your worst, Mr. Hughes.

INT./EXT. SIKORSKY AMPHIBIAN. NIGHT.

Night flying. There is nothing like it.

The stars and the moon glimmer above and the lights of Los Angeles glimmer below. The whole world seems an ebony ribbon with no horizon. It is dangerous and utterly free.

HOWARD pilots the Sikorsky, **KATE** in the co-pilot's seat next to him.

He soars down, swooping dangerously close over the roofs of some houses in the Hollywood Hills, buzzing them.

> HOWARD
> That's Mr. Mayer . . . Do you know where Jack Warner lives?

She laughs. She is entranced. Alive. Her senses tingling with every new sensation.

Her eye is drawn to the wheel ahead of her. There is something a bit peculiar about it. It is wrapped in cellophane. She touches the crinkly cellophane.

> KATE
> What's this on the steering wheel?

> HOWARD
> Cellophane . . . If you had any idea of the crap people carry around on their hands.

> KATE
> What kind of "crap"?

> HOWARD
> You don't want to know . . . Hold onto the wheel a bit. Get a feel for it. Don't worry, I've got the plane.

She takes the wheel ahead of her firmly.

> HOWARD
> (smiles)
> Too hard . . . Relax your hand . . . *(he shows her)* . . . You want to feel the vibration of the engine through your fingertips . . . You feel that?

> KATE
> Yes.

                    HOWARD

That's good . . . *(he takes his hands off his wheel)* . . . She's all yours.

                     KATE

Golly . . . *(he stands)* . . . Where are you going?!

                    HOWARD

I think there's some milk back there. You just keep us steady.

He moves to the rear of the plane and searches for a bottle of milk as she flies the plane. He watches her. Smiles. She absolutely loves it. Total control.

                     KATE

Howard, there's a rather alarming mountain heading our way.

                    HOWARD

Pull back on the wheel a smidge.

She pulls back the wheel and soars over some hills.

                     KATE

Golly!

He returns to his seat with a bottle of milk as:

                    HOWARD

I've never met anyone who actually says "Golly." You want me to take over?

                     KATE

Just when I'm getting the hang of it?

He smiles as she pilots the plane.

He looks at her, then at the bottle of milk. A beat. Should he do it?

####### HOWARD
Want some milk?

####### KATE
Please.

He carefully brings the milk bottle to her lips. She drinks. A bit of milk trickles down her chin. He gently wipes it away.

Then he returns to his seat. Looks at the milk bottle for a beat. And then takes a drink.

They sit, content in silence, as they soar through the night.

EXT. WILSHIRE COUNTRY CLUB. DAWN.

The Sikorsky is coming in for a landing, quite improbably heading toward the fairways of the Wilshire Country Club.

The plane sweeps between some impossibly tight trees—barely wide enough—and rolls to a stop in the middle of a fairway. Houses can be seen in the distance at the edge of the fairway.

HOWARD and **KATE** emerge.

####### KATE
. . . Utterly smashing! We'll do it again. I'm free Wednesday. A little early for golf though, don't you think?

####### HOWARD
No, I live here. Would you like a drink?

####### KATE
Lead on.

Howard leads her toward his house, a lovely affair on the edge of the golf course. She glances back at the plane in the middle of the fairway:

                             KATE
    Now that makes for a challenging par four.

He laughs and helps **KATE** over some low shrubs to his backyard, the Sikorsky remains behind them as if it were a car casually parked in his driveway.

INT. MUIRFIELD—LIVING ROOM. DAWN.

HOWARD's house, on Muirfield Drive in Hancock Park, is refined. Too refined for **HOWARD**.

HOWARD prepares a drink for **KATE**. They have comfortably switched roles: he is talking and she is watching.

                             HOWARD
    ... My decorator picked out the wallpaper and such. I hate
    this room. Gives me the willies. Like I'm about to be swal-
    lowed up by the latest issue of TOWN AND COUNTRY—

She strides across the room, without a word, and kisses him deeply. On her terms. He is surprised. Responds. She gently pulls her lips away, only inches from his:

                             KATE
    What room *do* you like?

                             HOWARD
    My study.

                             KATE
    Take me there . . .

She kisses him again . . . they kiss as he leads her through the house . . . they float through the house, little kisses and embraces along the way . . .

                              HOWARD
             You're the tallest woman I know . . .

                              KATE
             And all sharp elbows and knees, beware . . .

They continue to kiss as they move through the house, flowing effortlessly around each other . . .

                              KATE
             Will you fly me to work tomorrow?

                              HOWARD
             It is tomorrow.

They kiss their way into . . .

INT. MUIRFIELD—DEN. DAWN.

. . . **HOWARD**'s inner sanctum. The beating heart of the Muirfield house.

Dark, wood-paneled walls. Film editing machines and banks of electronics equipment. A huge desk with several phones, all of which have amplifiers to help with his deafness. French doors open to the spacious backyard and, beyond that, the fairways of the Wilshire Country Club.

HOWARD and **KATE** swirl around each other, their passion building. She is confident and enjoys him. He finds a powerful release in her firm touch.

There is no hesitation, no games. It is a passionate connection. It is honest.

His fingertips glide over her skin, imperceptibly taking us to . . .

INT. H-1 AIRPLANE HANGAR. DAY.

. . . **HOWARD**'s fingertips glide over the smooth, silver skin of the H-1.

GLENN and the engineers await his verdict. Incredibly tense.

HOWARD ducks down and continues to feel along the underside of the fuselage. His fingers glide slowly. He sweeps up again and completes his inspection, continuing to the tail of the racer.

He stands. Looks at the others. Smiles.

EXT. MARTIN FIELD. DAY.

A more unlikely location for such an important moment in **HOWARD**'s life would be hard to imagine.

Martin Field is a crude landing strip near Santa Ana. Paltry beet fields surround the air strip. There is no crowd. No glamour. In the distance, a few bored pilots tinker with ancient planes by a primitive quonset hut "terminal."

Three official timers and a few associates stand by a red flag planted in the ground at one end of the dirt runway. Another red flag and timer can be seen in the distance down the runway.

Title: September 13, 1935.
National Aeronautic Association Speed Trial.

The H-1 defies the unimpressive surroundings. It shines in the sunlight, sleek and muscular in the exact perfect measure.

HOWARD walks with **GLENN** toward the plane:

> **GLENN**
> . . . Keep your eye on the fuel gauge—we have a minimum of fuel to keep her weight down. Two runs. That's it. After that, you're flying on vapors and then you crash and then you die.

                    HOWARD
Right.

                    GLENN
Just give her easy flying, don't worry about speed. Today is not about records . . . *(they arrive at the plane)* . . . Honest to God, I wish you'd let someone else take her up—you got 20 damn test pilots working for you—

                    HOWARD
Hell, why should I let someone else have all the fun?

Then, impulsively, he takes **GLENN**'s brown fedora and puts it on his head.

                    HOWARD
See ya in a bit.

And he climbs into the plane.

INT./EXT. H-1. DAY.

HOWARD settles into the tight cockpit. He fastens his shoulder harnesses as he gazes at an amazing array of toggles and dials ahead of him on the control panel.

He was born to sit in a cockpit like this. He is completely at home in the mad jumble of leather and steel and dials and switches. The complexity delights him. The options.

He slowly puts his hand around the stick, finger by finger. Getting a feel for the stick. Feels good.

Then he flicks the engine start toggles and pushes ignition. The plane's engine thunders to life. An elegant cascade of power. Outside, **GLENN** listens to the engine, eyes closed. Then he gives **HOWARD** the thumbs-up.

Inside, **HOWARD** responds and starts the plane moving.

This is foreplay. The H-1 rolls down the dirt landing strip. Reaches the end. Turns in one smooth motion.

HOWARD sees the strip ahead of him. Plenty long enough. He glances to the red flags. Hanging listlessly. No wind. Fine. He will do it without any help from the wind.

Stasis. He waits. The engine prepares. He prepares.

And then the most gentle pressure on the foot pedals and stick . . .

. . . And the H-1 begins to move. Gaining speed. **HOWARD** puts more pressure on the stick and throttle. The foreplay is over. Time to let the cat out of the bag. More pressure on the stick. His feet dance over the floor pedals.

It happens so quickly we are unprepared.

The H-1 accelerates in a *blinding silver flash*—engine singing—and is suddenly airborne.

The three timers from the National Aeronautic Association are absolutely stunned as the H-1 zooms past them, knocking their hats off.

GLENN smiles. **HOWARD**'s engineers and mechanics cheer.

HOWARD has never known acceleration like this! The cockpit is vibrating like mad. The needle falls off his compass. The world is shooting past him.

He puts his left hand on his right wrist, steadying his hand on the stick.

He banks the plane around, back toward the field, the earth rotating dramatically below him.

And he flies. Pure speed. He forces the stick. The engine rises to the challenge. His eyes dart over the dials. He sees the red flags below. First run.

Zip—and he is past them.

Below, the three timers click stopwatches.

HOWARD banks the plane again. Too sharply. The plane veers. He controls his energy. Levels out. Takes a breath. Zooms toward the red flags.

The air field nears. **HOWARD** plays the stick and throttle. The engine embraces his challenge. Second run.

Zip—and he is past them.

The stopwatches click.

GLENN breathes a sigh of relief.

But **HOWARD** is not done.

He takes the plane a little farther out this time. Banks around. He is comfortable now. Just getting the feel for the plane. Can't stop now. He knows what the plane likes. What gives it pleasure.

He very gently forces the stick and throttle a bit more—the engine responds to him—is that a roar of protest? or is it satisfaction? give me some more?—the whole world is vibrating madly now—another dial needle falls from the control panel.

The stick is bucking in his hand now—he uses both hands to steady it.

Third run.

The H-1 sweeps through the sky faster than any plane has ever flown.

Zip—and he is past them.

The stopwatches click.

HOWARD smiles.

                    HOWARD
    Good girl.

EXT. MARTIN FIELD. FOLLOWING.

The H-1 can be seen circling in the distance as **GLENN** hurries to the clutch of timers:

                    TIMER
    (stunned)
    352 miles per hour . . .

GLENN turns to the other engineers:

                    GLENN
    352!!

They cheer wildly—

INT./EXT. H-1. DAY.

HOWARD is returning to the field when—

There is an enormous thunk. The engine sputters to a stop. A red indicator light flashes. **HOWARD** doesn't need the light. He can see the propeller ahead of him stop spinning.

And it is suddenly silent. No engine roar. Just the gentle whoosh of the wind.

The plane begins to descend quickly. **HOWARD** tries to keep it level, truly fighting with the stick now.

The beet field beyond the air strip zooms up at him, inescapable. He braces himself with one arm as he fights with the stick to keep the nose up.

He is going to crash.

The bottom of the plane zips over the beets—slicing them to pieces—**HOWARD** keeps control, doesn't panic—keeps the nose up—

And the H-1 comes to earth.

A thundering bounce as she makes contact—**HOWARD** is jolted violently—his teeth slam together—his harness digs into him—the H-1 tears through the beet field—a propeller blade snaps off—it slices through the top of the cockpit—missing Howard by inches—

The H-1 continues to slide—the floor boards under **HOWARD**'s feet rip away, he raises his feet, a bit too late, one of his shoes is shredded—the H-1 continues to slide—

EXT. MARTIN FIELD. FOLLOWING.

GLENN and the engineers watch in stunned disbelief.

>   ENGINEER
> Well, there goes our meal ticket.

>   GLENN
> COME ON!

They race to waiting cars.

EXT. BEET FIELD. DAY.

The cars tear through the beet field, following the trail cut by the H-1. They slam to a stop.

GLENN climbs out. Can't believe what he sees.

HOWARD is sitting calmly on the engine cowl of the H-1, making notes. His lucky fedora pushed back on his head.

                    HOWARD
How'd we do?

                    GLENN
352 on the last run.

HOWARD continues to make notes, doesn't look up.

                    HOWARD
She'll go faster.

GLENN and the engineers move to the ravaged plane. And to the fastest man on the planet.

INT. MUIRFIELD. DAY.

HOWARD limps in, excited.

                    HOWARD
Kate! Katie!

                    KATE (V.O.)
Upstairs!

He hobbles through the house quickly, up the stairs to . . .

INT. MUIRFIELD-MASTER BEDROOM. DAY.

KATE is sitting on the bed reading a script, making notes, very much at home. **HOWARD** limps in.

                    KATE

Lord, what happened to you—?

                    HOWARD

Oh, nothing—hard landing. Cut my foot. You'll—

                    KATE

Sit down, I'll take care of it. Tell me everything!

He sits and carefully removes his shredded shoe as she goes to the bathroom to get antiseptic and bandages.

                    HOWARD

You can't imagine what it was like, Katie! You can't imagine the speed—she was fine, just fine!

                    KATE

(from bathroom)
What'd she make?

                    HOWARD

Oh . . . around . . . 352.

She emerges from the bathroom, stunned.

                    KATE

You did it.

                    HOWARD

Fastest man on the planet.

She races to him and kisses him, joyous—

KATE

Oh, well done! I'm so proud of you—!

HOWARD

She did it, baby.

KATE

Now let me see your foot—Good God you're covered in blood!

HOWARD

No, that's beet juice. I crashed in a beet field.

She looks at his red, beet juice-covered foot for a beat. And then laughs. As does he. The absurdity of **HOWARD**'s grand adventure killing them.

KATE

Here let me get you fixed up—Heavens, what is this, electrical tape?

She begins trying to clean the small cut on the sole of his foot as:

HOWARD

Odie just sorta slammed it on—wanted to get home to tell you.

KATE

I'm so proud of you—this is going to sting a little bit—*(he winces as she cleans the wound)*—this is useless, come to the bathroom. And don't get beet juice on the carpet!

She helps him hop into . . .

INT. MUIRFIELD-MASTER BATH. FOLLOWING.

KATE

Sit down.

He sits on the edge of the tub. She turns on the tap and carefully cleans the beet juice off his foot.

                    HOWARD
Too hot!

                    KATE
Don't be a baby. Was the press there?

                    HOWARD
No, they're calling everyone.

She turns off the tap and begins cleaning his wound.

                    HOWARD
Should be on the wires by now . . . *(a beat)* . . . What is it?

A beat as she gently cleans his wound.

                    HOWARD
Kate?

She begins to carefully dress his wound, deep in thought.

                    KATE
I've been famous—for better or worse—for a long time now . . . I wonder if you know what that really means.

                    HOWARD
I got my fair share of press on HELL'S ANGELS. I'm used to it.

                    KATE
Are you?

She stops dressing his wound. Considering whether to go on. She will. She sits back, leaning against a bathroom wall, looking at him deeply.

KATE

Howard, we're not like everyone else. Too many sharp angles. Too many eccentricities. We have to be very careful not to let people in or they'll make us into freaks.

HOWARD

Katie, they can't get in here. We're safe.

KATE

They can always get in . . . When my brother killed himself there were photographers at the funeral . . . There's no decency to it.

She resumes dressing his wound.

A long beat. He is deep in thought.

HOWARD

(very quietly)
Look at me, Katie . . .

She stops dressing his wound and looks at him.

He is completely honest. Completely vulnerable.

HOWARD

Sometimes I feel like . . . well, I get these ideas . . . crazy ideas about things that may not really be there . . .

KATE

Howard . . .

HOWARD

. . . Sometimes I truly fear I'm losing my mind . . . Do you understand? . . . If I did, it would be like flying blind, with no compass, no window.

She takes his hand.

> KATE
> You taught me to fly, Howard. I'll take the wheel.

He holds her closely, desperately.

INT. JUAN TRIPPE'S OFFICE—PAN AM. DAY.

A globe. The world. **JUAN TRIPPE**'s world.

We take in the globe as we hear a radio news report, there is a roaring crowd in the background of the radio report:

> RADIO ANNOUNCER (V.O.)
> . . . Yes, young Howard Hughes has done it!—Flown all the way around the entire world in three days and nineteen hours. Beating Wiley Post's record by almost half! American's Number One Aviation Hero is now the Fastest Man on the Planet . . . !

We discover the mammoth globe fills the center of **TRIPPE**'s New York office. It deserves to. Pan Am is Tiffany's when everyone else in the game is Woolworth's.

The familiar blue-and-white Pan Am logo looms behind . . .

Title: Juan Trippe. President of Pan Am Airways.

JUAN TRIPPE sits behind his desk, smoking a pipe, doing paperwork. The radio is on his desk.

TRIPPE is every inch the elite Yale graduate. He was born to wear tweed and he does. He is one of the true fathers of commercial aviation; the unquestioned overlord of Pan Am, America's only international airline.

He is brilliant, innovative and lethal. He will soon become **HOWARD**'s absolute nemesis.

The radio report continues to declaim **HOWARD**'s triumph. **TRIPPE** rather sourly turns it off. Click.

He continues to work in silence. Then an **EXECUTIVE** enters. **TRIPPE** casts a baleful eye up to the interruption.

> EXECUTIVE
> You're not going to believe this. Just came over the wires . . . Howard Hughes just bought control of TWA.

A beat as **TRIPPE** looks at him.

> TRIPPE
> I thought Mr. Hughes was flying around the world?

> EXECUTIVE
> Apparently he did while he was flying—over the radio.

TRIPPE is impressed with **HOWARD**'s panache. He thinks.

> TRIPPE
> I've heard some . . . disquieting rumors about Mr. Hughes. I'd certainly like to know everything there is to know about Mr. Hughes . . . Attend to it. Thoroughly.

He returns to his paperwork.

EXT. PANTAGES THEATER. NIGHT.

A sudden attack of flashbulbs. A brutal machine gun assault.

HOWARD and **KATE** are trapped on the red carpet outside a movie premiere at the glorious Pantages. He endures the attack. She seems to enjoy it.

A cacophony of voices. Gossip hounds and fans and reporters and photographers:

> VOICES
> HOWARD!—MISS HEPBURN!—WHEN YA GONNA NAME THE DAY, HOWARD?!—WHAT ABOUT GINGER ROGERS?!—HOWARD!—MR. HUGHES!

He does his best to smile. To survive. He notes **KATE** posing, bending to the photographers slightly, giving them her best side, showing off her gown to the best advantage. Her eyes seem immune to the cruel flashes.

But the photographers aren't much interested in her. They point their cameras at **HOWARD**, continuing to call questions to him.

He pulls at her arm a bit, wanting to go. She resists.

He waits for her performance to end.

One fact is glaringly obvious: they are all more interested in **HOWARD** than in her.

INT. PANTAGES THEATER—LOBBY. NIGHT.

Finally through the doors, **HOWARD** escorts **KATE** through the lobby.

> KATE
> You know fame is supposed to be my turf.

She sees **LOUIS B. MAYER** standing with a pack of his MGM cronies. She pulls her arm away from **HOWARD** and floats to **MAYER**.

HOWARD stands for a moment, lost, watching her. She sparkles for **MAYER**.

Then a bewitching form floats past **HOWARD**, voice purring:

                              AVA
Don't worry, Howard, she's just working the room . . .

AVA GARDNER is the most beautiful woman in the world. A siren. A tigress. Currently on the arm of a movie executive.

                              AVA
It's her job, baby.

She winks to **HOWARD** and continues into the theater.

HOWARD watches **KATE** with **MAYER** and his cronies. They laugh. Glance in his direction. **KATE** is being very amusing about something.

HOWARD'S POV-EXTREME CLOSEUP—**KATE** and **MAYER**—laughing, open mouths, eyes looking at him—his deafness is overpowering, he can't hear what they are saying.

His paranoia is extreme. It is unbearable. He escapes to the bathroom.

INT. PANTAGES THEATER-MEN'S ROOM. FOLLOWING.

HOWARD goes to a row of shining sinks. He reaches into his jacket pocket and removes a small cake of lye soap. Carefully unwraps it. Then begins to wash his hands.

A toilet flushes in a stall behind him. He glances back in the mirror. An unusual amount of movement inside the stall. He continues to look in the mirror as he washes his hands, curious.

Then the stall door opens and a **MAN** lurches out of the stall awkwardly. He is on arm crutches. Polio.

HOWARD watches as the **MAN** jerks his way across the room, slowly nearing the sink next to him. **HOWARD** is trapped.

                    POLIO MAN
Hello.

                     HOWARD
Hello.

HOWARD watches as the **MAN** washes his hands, leaning forward on his arm crutches.

                    POLIO MAN
Could you reach me a towel?

HOWARD turns. A neat stack of white towels next to him.

He turns back to the **MAN**.

                     HOWARD
I can't really do that. I'm sorry.

The **MAN** looks at him. Okay. He jerks his way past **HOWARD** and dries his hands.

HOWARD looks away. Focusing on his washing his hands.

The **MAN** jerks his way out of the bathroom. **HOWARD** lets out a few deep breaths.

INT. PANTAGES-LOBBY. FOLLOWING.

HOWARD emerges from the men's room. **KATE** is waiting.

                      KATE
I'm an idiot and I'm sorry.

                     HOWARD
(smiles)
Forget it—

                         KATE

I'm a vain, preening ass without a single redeeming feature.

                        HOWARD

That's not fair. You have very good teeth.

She laughs. He offers his arm to lead her into the auditorium.

                        HOWARD

Come on . . .

                         KATE

I have a better idea. Take me flying. Better yet, I'll take you flying.

                        HOWARD

Do your worst, Miss Hepburn.

They leave the theater. The flashbulbs explode again as they go.

INT. CAR-FENWICK. DAY.

Something we have never seen in this story. Fall. Yellow and red leaves.

New England.

HOWARD and **KATE** are driving up the long drive to a huge house. It is Fenwick. The Hepburns' ancestral Connecticut manor and home to **KATE**'s patrician Yankee clan.

                         KATE

Don't be so squirmy, Howard. You're going to get on famously with mother and father. And I'm almost sure they'll like you too. Once they get to know you.

He glances at her.

Ahead of them **HOWARD** can see the Hepburns cavorting about the huge lawn as they approach. Pedigree dogs run hither and yon. Servants scurry here and there. Other kinfolk, extended relations, play croquet enthusiastically.

The robust **MRS. HEPBURN** appears to be doing something like calisthenics. Or perhaps dancing. **HOWARD**'s not quite sure.

The slightly more reserved **DR. HEPBURN** is painting on the porch.

Another **MAN** is happily filming everything with a home movie camera. He swings the camera toward the car as it approaches.

> HOWARD
>
> Who's that with the camera?

> KATE
>
> My ex-husband, Ludlow. Mother and father are mad about Luddy.

> HOWARD
>
> What the hell's he doing here?!

> KATE
>
> Oh, he's here all the time.

HOWARD stops the car and **KATE** leaps out . . .

EXT. FENWICK. FOLLOWING.

KATE floats from the car and embraces her parents, snapping into a heightened and arch persona appropriate to her family. Her usual role with them. **LUDLOW** films. Then he turns the camera to **HOWARD**.

> KATE
>
> Hepburns! Hepburns! Attention please! . . . Everyone! This . . . is Howard!

A huge Great Dane races up and leaps on **HOWARD**.

Welcome to Fenwick where all the blood is blue and all the jaws are clenched.

INT. FENWICK-DINING ROOM. NIGHT.

Everyone is talking at once. And all very quickly.

The huge Great Dane has taken quite a shine to **HOWARD**. It sleeps across one of his feet under the table. Trapping him.

Dinner at the Hepburn's is a thrilling experience, if you like juggling axes blindfolded.

                        MRS. HEPBURN

... We pay our devotion to the arts here. A colony we have created. Julian is a painter—(**HOWARD** looks around, who the hell is Julian?)—abstract of course. What the hell's the point of painting something real when you can just take a picture nowadays, don't you agree? Where do you stand on politics, Mr. Hughes?

                        HOWARD

Excuse me?

                        MRS. HEPBURN

We're all socialists here!

                        KATE

We are not.

                        MRS. HEPBURN

Yes, I've said it! Sacco and Vanzetti and all that! Now you've met Mr. Roosevelt, what make you of him?

The Great Dane beneath **HOWARD** grunts and rolls over. Trapping both feet. **HOWARD** winces.

> LUDLOW

What are you sniggering at?

> HOWARD

Excuse me?

> LUDLOW

You just sniggered.

> HOWARD

No, the dog. It's crushing my feet.

> DR. HEPBURN

Don't you like dogs?

> MRS. HEPBURN

Young man, I will not have sniggering at Mr. Roosevelt at my table. Please leave.

> HOWARD

I wasn't.

> DR. HEPBURN

I thought everybody liked dogs.

> MRS. HEPBURN

Perhaps he had a bad experience as a child?

> LUDLOW

Katie, does it stick in your craw that Howard here gets more press than you do?

                    DR. HEPBURN
A bad experience with a dog?

                    KATE
It's a blessed relief, I can tell you! Cameras out of my mug for once.

                    LUDLOW
What a shy creature you are.

They laugh.

HOWARD'S POV—EXTREME CLOSEUP—all those talking faces-the mountains of food, blood dripping from the too rare roast beef, the sickly and glistening vegetables—

As the almost incomprehensible chatter of so many voices all talking at once continues like a firestorm—

                    MRS. HEPBURN
          (continuing to **DR. HEPBURN***)*
Perhaps it was a particularly large dog?

                    KATE
          (continuing to **LUDLOW***)*
Oh, it's all very well for you to make fun, but the press can be a damned nuisance when you just want to do your job.

                    DR. HEPBURN
Like a Doberman? Was it a Doberman, Mr. Hughes? Or a dachshund?!

                    KATE
It's like the press think they own you.

                    LUDLOW
They should all be lined up against a wall and shot. Like in that Spanish painting, you know . . .

                    MRS. HEPBURN
Dachshunds are little dogs, dear.

                    KATE
Goya! The Goya painting!

                    LUDLOW
Of course. Mexicans I think, poor lambs.

                    DR. HEPBURN
We're not shooting anyone. Not even the press. And anyway . . .

HOWARD forces himself to concentrate, tears himself back to reality as:

                    DR. HEPBURN
. . . that's the vulgar press, I'm sure. Read much, Mr. Hughes?

                    HOWARD
I try to stay up to snuff on the trade journals.

                    ANOTHER GUEST
Snuff?

                    MRS. HEPBURN
These would be flying magazines?

                    HOWARD
Sorry?

                    KATE
He's a little deaf.

MRS. HEPBURN

(louder)
You read flying magazines?

HOWARD

Trade journals on engineering. Aviation.

MRS. HEPBURN

We read books.

KATE

(apologizing for **HOWARD***)*
Howard has to read the trade pieces because he's designing a new airplane.

LUDLOW

(not remotely interested)
Do tell.

At last, something he can talk about.

HOWARD

Well, it's pretty exciting actually. It's a spy plane for the Air Corps. A twin-engine plane with some really interesting design features, it has two booms at the back, which is—

MRS. HEPBURN

Luddy built a bird house once. You remember that, dear?

LUDLOW

A mere trifle, darling.

ANOTHER GUEST

Goya is vastly overrated. All the Spaniards are!

KATE

Nonsense—Picasso is sacred!

DR. HEPBURN
(*conspiratorially to* **HOWARD**)
I'm a urologist.

KATE
A "sacred monster" that's what Picasso is. That's Cocteau's phrase for Piaf, of course, but doesn't it fit?

MRS. HEPBURN
It was quite aesthetic really. Birds didn't care for it much, but the bats do.

HOWARD
I'll bet.

MRS. HEPBURN
Do speak up, dear.

HOWARD
Nothing.

MRS. HEPBURN
Then why did you speak? I can't abide people who speak but have nothing to say.

HOWARD glances to **KATE**, she offers no assistance.

LUDLOW
Did you go to mechanic school to learn all this airplane guff?

HOWARD
No.

KATE
God, don't get him started on airplanes!

DR. HEPBURN
Or dogs, apparently. He had a bad experience with a dachshund.

LUDLOW
Then how did you make all that money?

MRS. HEPBURN
We don't care about money here, Mr. Hughes.

HOWARD
(*terse*)
That's because you have it.

A beat. An actual moment of silence.

MRS. HEPBURN
Would you repeat that?

HOWARD
You don't care about money because you have it. And you've always had it. My father was dirt poor when I was born—

LUDLOW
Back in torrid Houston would this be?

HOWARD
Excuse me!—(*back to Mrs. Hepburn*)—I care about money, because I know what it takes out of a man to make it. Now if you'll excuse me, I have some "airplane guff" to take care of.

He tosses down his napkin, wrenches his feet from under the dog, and strides out of the room.

The **HEPBURNS** consider.

LUDLOW
Seems rather a highly strung chap.

                         KATE
          You're a fine bunch of bullies, aren't you?

They continue eating. **HOWARD** is quickly forgotten by all.

                      DR. HEPBURN
Have you talked to Mr. Mayer about letting you do JANE
EYRE?

                         KATE
Old cretin won't budge. Too "arty" don't you know. I'm convinced the man hasn't read anything longer than a Sunday "Katzenjammer Kids" in his life . . .

EXT. FENWICK—FRONT LAWN. NIGHT.

A bit later. **HOWARD** stands on front lawn, deep in thought. He aimlessly kicks a croquet ball. It rolls through a hoop.

                      KATE'S VOICE
          No fair kicking, you have to use the mallet.

She comes to him.

                         KATE
Really, though, you can't retire from the field of battle like that or they'll never respect you.

                        HOWARD
Katie . . . I don't understand. You were like a different person in there.

                         KATE
They just expect me to be a certain way . . . But there's only one real Kate. Your Kate.

She kisses him and they head back toward the house.

INT. 7000 ROMAINE—SCREENING ROOM. DAY.

JANE RUSSELL, larger than life, is pressing in on us, her breasts threatening to devour us. Again and again. Dailies from THE OUTLAW.

HOWARD sits, drawing something we do not see on a pad. He occasionally glances up at the footage. His filmmaking team sits behind him. **GLENN** and some engineers sit before him.

> HOWARD
> ... Edison used to say you never invented anything until there was a need for it—well, there's a *need* for this. You know how many Allied ships we lost this year because of U-Boat attacks?

> GLENN
> No.

> HOWARD
> 681 ships, just this year, so far. The Army *needs* a new plane to fly the troops over to Europe. Ships are always gonna be too vulnerable to the U-boats.

> GLENN
> You wanna build a troop carrier plane?

> HOWARD
> Stop thinking like an insect, Odie. Not just a plane to carry troops—a plane to carry *everything*! The troops and the tanks and the jeeps and whatnot . . .

He pulls a folded-over headshot of a starlet from his jacket and hands it to **GLENN**.

> HOWARD
> Take a look—other side.

GLENN flips the headshot over. And we see a pencil drawing **HOWARD** has done of a new plane. A gigantic flying boat.

We recognize it instantly. The Hercules. The Spruce Goose.

               GLENN
Oh shit . . .

               HOWARD
Say 200 feet from nose to tail. Wingspan around 300. It's gonna need around 24,000 horsepower—

               GLENN
Oh shit!

               HOWARD
This is just what Kaiser and the Army are looking for—don't worry, they'll pay for it.

               GLENN
Christ, Howard, what are you getting us into?!

               HOWARD
So it's a big plane. That's why I'm calling it The Hercules. That's a swell name isn't it?

               GLENN
How heavy do you imagine this thing is?

               HOWARD
I'd say around 200 tons.

GLENN is staggered. A 200 ton plane?!

               HOWARD
I didn't say it was going to be easy.

He finally completes what he has been drawing, he turns and shows it to the filmmaking team behind him. It is a very good engineering drawing of an underwire bra.

> HOWARD
> Rig up something like this, should give the proper uplift ratios while reducing the need for additional torque support on the front. I want smooth titties, gentlemen.

He turns back to **GLENN** with a smile:

> HOWARD
> It's all engineering, isn't it, Odie?

GLENN considers **JANE RUSSELL**'s breasts on the screen.

> GLENN
> Howard, you really think they're gonna let you put out a whole movie just about tits?

> HOWARD
> Sure, who doesn't like tits?

Cut to—

INT. MPA HEARING ROOM. DAY.

Ten somber men in somber double-breasted suits.

Men who decidedly do not like tits.

Title: Motion Picture Association Censorship Board.

PROFESSOR FITZ, HOWARD's meteorologist, sits nervously at a long table before the panel of somber men. He has no idea why he is here.

A number of large easels have been set up at the back of the room, facing the panel. The easels apparently contain huge posters or something. Covered in sheets.

A silent beat as the panel gazes at poor **PROFESSOR FITZ**.

Then **HOWARD** sweeps in and sits. Brisk.

> HOWARD
> Good afternoon, gentlemen. Sorry I'm late.

> CHAIRMAN
> Will the secretary record that Mr. Hughes has arrived and this session will now be called to order. I yield the floor to Mr. Breen.

JOSEPH BREEN, Hollywood's censorship czar, stands.

> BREEN
> Mr. Hughes, members of the committee... I have reviewed Mr. Hughes' photoplay entitled THE OUTLAW and can state categorically that I have never seen anything quite so unacceptable as the shots of the mammaries of the character named "Rio." Throughout almost half the picture the girl's mammaries, which are quite large and prominent, are shockingly uncovered. For this reason I have concluded that the picture appeals only to prurient interest and should be denied the Motion Picture Association's Seal of Approval.

He sits.

> CHAIRMAN
> Thank you, Mr. Breen... Mr. Hughes you may address the committee.

HOWARD
(*stands*)

Thank you, Mr. Chairman. Mr. Breen . . . Now the situation here seems to revolve around Miss Russell's "mammaries." Mr. Breen feels that they are too prominent. More prominent than other "mammaries" have been on the screen. With the help of my associate here I hope to dispel that notion . . .

He goes to the easels at the back of the room. Begins pulling off the sheets, one by one.

Each easel contains a huge, enlarged photograph of breasts and cleavage. Just breasts and cleavage. No heads.

HOWARD
Jean Harlow . . . Ann Sheridan . . . Irene Dunne . . . Claudette Colbert . . . Rita Hayworth . . . Betty Grable . . . and Jane Russell.

The panel members gape. **PROFESSOR FITZ** gapes.

HOWARD
Now all these shots, save for Miss Russell, were enlarged from pictures that received Mr. Breen's Seal of Approval. As you have probably noticed by now, they all contain "mammaries." I will ask my associate to join me now . . .

PROFESSOR FITZ rises and walks to **HOWARD** and the mammaries, completely confused.

HOWARD
May I introduce Dr. Ludlow Branson from Columbia University. He's a mathematician of some note. Dr. Branson will now demonstrate that, in fact, Miss Russell's "mammaries" are no more prominent than any of these other fine ladies.

He hands the stunned **PROFESSOR FITZ** a pair of calipers from his pocket.

                        HOWARD
You forgot your calipers, Doctor.

HOWARD returns to his seat. **PROFESSOR FITZ** improvises:

                    PROFESSOR FITZ
Well . . . gentlemen . . . ah . . . you'll see that in, um, mammary exhibit number one the length of the actual, cleavage, if I may, is . . . *(he uses the calipers)* . . . Five inches and quarter . . . Now if we go to, um, mammary exhibit number two we will find . . .

PROFESSOR FITZ proceeds gamely. **HOWARD** watches him. Smiles.

As we hear an amplified voice:

                      EMCEE (V.O.)
. . . pleased to bring you The Wonder of Modern Aviation . . .

INT. NIGHTCLUB. EVENING.

It's like a trade show. With one vendor.

An EMCEE stands before a microphone on a stage at one end of the room. A red velvet curtain emblazoned with "Hughes Aircraft" hangs across the stage, concealing something.

A gaggle of reporters wait.

As does the all-important delegation from the Air Corps. Seven men in uniform. Each is with a beautiful, younger woman.

These seven men will decide whether or not to fund the project.

EMCEE
... Not just a plane, ladies and gentlemen, a vast leap forward in aeronautic technology. But it's more than that. It's our humble gesture to the war effort, our chance to help out those brave men in uniform ...

The **EMCEE** continues to ballyhoo as we find **HOWARD** in a corner, standing with **JOHNNY MEYER**.

HOWARD's eyes never leave the delegation from the Air Corps.

HOWARD
... and every bill comes to me. They don't pay for anything. Those men decide whether or not to fund the plane, so I need them real happy, do what it takes.

JOHNNY
You got it.

HOWARD
What about the girls?

JOHNNY
Let's put it this way ... I don't think the gentlemen from the Air Corps will have any trouble scoring tonight.

The **EMCEE** continues:

EMCEE
... And now let me introduce you to the creator of this magnificent airplane. You know him as an aviator, an industrialist, an American hero. We here at Hughes Aircraft just know him as a patriot. Ladies and gentlemen ... Howard Hughes.

The crowd applauds. **HOWARD** joins the **EMCEE** on the stage. He looks out over the sea of faces. Doesn't know quite what to say. Settles for:

                                HOWARD
Well, let's see her.

Gorgeous starlets emerge and slowly pull back the red curtain to reveal . . .

The Hercules.

History will come to know it as The Spruce Goose.

A huge silver model of the gigantic flying boat slowly revolves, a glowing Art Deco sign flashing "The Hercules" behind it. Gasps from the crowd. Flashbulbs. But **HOWARD** only has eyes for the Air Corps delegation. Are they impressed? Will they pay?

The **EMCEE** leans into the microphone:

                                EMCEE
Imagine, if you dare, this beautiful lady towering over your head. And inside? 700 brave American soldiers! A dozen Sherman tanks! All winging their way over the Atlantic free from the threat of the U-boats prowling the icy waters below. Imagine a fleet of these planes . . .

He continues to extol the virtues of the Hercules.

HOWARD notes one of the women with one of the Air Corps officers. She puts her hand on his arm, whispers into his ear. He smiles.

HOWARD knows. They'll pay.

INT. MUIRFIELD—HALLWAY. NIGHT.

The cover of HOLLYWOOD EXPOSE magazine, a sleazy rag showing a picture of Howard with various female movie stars. The bold cover title: THE MANY LOVES OF HOWARD HUGHES.

As we hear **KATE**:

> KATE (V.O.)
> ... don't you see how degrading this is for me?!

HOWARD is roaming, eating vanilla ice cream straight from the carton as **KATE** follows. She holds the magazine. Furious.

> KATE
> Don't you see how this demeans me?!

> HOWARD
> Since when do you care about the scandal rags?

> KATE
> Every time there's a picture of you with another woman it's like a slap in the face, don't you understand that?!

> HOWARD
> That's overstating it a bit, don't ya think?

> KATE
> *(brandishing magazine)*
> Joan Crawford, Ginger Rogers, Linda Darnell. Joan Fontaine ... and now *Bette Davis* for God's sake!

> HOWARD
> They're Cracker Jack candy, honey. You know they don't mean anything—

> KATE
> Oh, very nice.

> HOWARD
> You're the one who said all men are predators. It's all in Darwin, remember?

He goes into the den, she follows . . .

INT. MUIRFIELD—DEN. FOLLOWING.

KATE
And am I to expect this to continue after the wedding?

HOWARD
What's really bothering you? Is it the women or the publicity?

She finally explodes:

KATE
CAN'T YOU EAT ICE CREAM FROM A BOWL LIKE EVERYONE ELSE IN THE WORLD?!

The phone on **HOWARD**'s desk rings.

KATE
Don't you dare.

He answers the phone. She is stunned.

HOWARD (ON PHONE)
Yeah?—This isn't a good time, Odie . . . What? . . . *(he is now completely focused on the phone conversation)* . . . For Christ sake we can't make the Hercules if we can't get any aluminum. Wait . . . *(he turns up the amplifier on his phone so he can hear better)* . . . Yeah, I can hear you now . . . No—you tell the War Production Board this *is* an essential strategic operation and . . . No . . .

KATE steams.

HOWARD (ON PHONE)
. . . Look, if they're giving aluminum to Douglas and Northrop and Boeing they sure as hell can give some to Hughes Aircraft . . .

                            KATE
    Don't set the ice cream—

He sets the messy ice cream carton on his desk. She knows it will leave a ring. Intolerable.

                       HOWARD (ON PHONE)
    ... Meantime, we gotta think of something else. If we can't
    get any aluminum we'll have to find another way ... Christ, I
    don't know, find some alloy that works as well, you tell me ...
    Right ...

He continues on the phone. She stalks out.

INT. LARGE SEDAN—MGM. DAY.

HOWARD and KATE sit in the rear of a large sedan. HOWARD talks to GLENN in the front seat. A large Cuban man we will come to know as JORGE drives. They are driving through the MGM lot.

We watch KATE's face. Clouded. Sad. Deep in thought.

                            HOWARD
    ... Dammit, Odie, if we can't get any aluminum we'll use
    wood.

                            GLENN
    You can't make a 200 ton plane out of wood.

                            HOWARD
    Why the hell not?! The damn thing's a flying *boat*. What did
    they use to make boats out of?! Think of the Hercules like a
    Spanish Galleon—a goddamn flying Spanish Galleon!

They pull up to KATE's trailer. He kisses her cheek.

HOWARD
I love you honey . . . *(he continues to Glenn as she climbs out of the car)* . . . we just gotta find the right kind of wood—something light but strong—with the tensile properties to work with the Duramold bonding . . .

EXT. MGM LOT. DAY.

The sedan pulls away as **KATE** goes into her trailer . . .

INT. KATE'S TRAILER. DAY.

SPENCER TRACY is sitting comfortably rumpled and relaxed in her trailer. He tosses her an apple. She catches it.

SPENCER TRACY
From my farm. If you like it I'll get you a bushel.

She takes a bite of the apple. Tears come to her eyes.

SPENCER TRACY
Trouble with Mr. Hughes?

KATE
There's too much Howard Hughes in Howard Hughes. That's the trouble.

INT. HUGHES AIRCRAFT-XF-11 HANGAR. NIGHT.

The new plane is brilliantly illuminated.

It is **HOWARD**'s new twin-engine reconnaissance plane. Even in this incomplete state the XF-11 is dramatic. Twin rear booms flanking a needle-nosed cockpit. 65 feet long with a wingspan of 101 feet. Extremely graceful lines, smooth surfaces and streamlined elegance.

The hangar is empty but for **HOWARD**. He stands at the plane, working, arms thrust into the guts of the engine.

A radio plays Christmas carols.

> JACK (V.O.)
> Beautiful . . .

HOWARD turns, **JACK FRYE** has just entered the hangar with **ROBERT GROSS**, the dignified President of Lockheed. They are gazing at the new plane, dazzled.

HOWARD goes to them, cleaning his hands on a rag.

> GROSS
> *(smiles)*
> Don't you even take Christmas off?

GROSS offers his hand.

Title: Robert Gross. President of Lockheed Aircraft.

> HOWARD
> *(not shaking)*
> Sorry, got grease on my hands. Nice to see you, Bob.

He holds up his finger for them to be quiet. Then turns up the radio so they can't be overheard.

> HOWARD
> Take a look . . . She's the XF-11 reconnaissance flier, spy plane really. Her top speed is 450—which means she can outrun anything they throw against her. After the Japs stole my H-1 design for their goddamn Zeros, I figured I needed to do 'em one better. Designed every inch of her myself.

GROSS
She's a looker.

HOWARD
Okay, what have you got for me?

GROSS carries something covered in a cloth to a drafting table. He pulls off the cloth, revealing a model of an airplane. The Constellation.

If the XF-11 is a radical design, the airplane model before **HOWARD** is nothing short of revolutionary.

The plane's shape is dolphin-like, elegantly dipping down at the nose and then sloping up to the three vertical tail wings. Four engines.

HOWARD almost gasps.

HOWARD
Jiminy Cricket . . .

GROSS
Seating capacity for 60. Wingspan 123 feet. Four Double Cyclone engines. Her ceiling is 25,000 feet.

HOWARD
(studies the model)
Gross weight?

GROSS
86,000. Wing load to 41 pounds psi.

HOWARD
Less drag on the plane in thinner air, so at full mix you're looking at a top speed of—(instantly does the math)—around 340, giving her a range of about . . .

HOWARD stops. A stunning realization.

> HOWARD
>
> 3,000 miles.

He looks up at them. 3,000 miles. The magic number.

> HOWARD
>
> Cross country.

> JACK
>
> Non-stop.

HOWARD continues to look at them. 3,000 miles. The sacred number.

Then he looks more closely at **GROSS**.

> HOWARD
>
> You have something on your suit.

> GROSS
>
> What?

> HOWARD
>
> On your lapel, there's something on your lapel.

> GROSS
> *(looking)*
> Where?

HOWARD hands him a handkerchief from his pocket.

> HOWARD
>
> Right there. Clean it off, would ya?

GROSS cleans a speck of lint off his lapel. Offers the handkerchief back.

HOWARD
Throw it away . . . (GROSS *moves to a nearby trash can*) . . . No, over there.

GROSS tosses the handkerchief into a trash can a little further away.

HOWARD
So what do you call her?

GROSS
The Constellation, but we can change that.

HOWARD
No, it's pretty.

HOWARD tucks his hands into his pockets and walks away, deep in thought.

HOWARD
I like her . . . (*he glances in the trash can where* **GROSS** *threw the handkerchief, disquieted*) . . . What kind of deal can you give me? . . . (*he repeats the movement and words exactly, looking into the trash can again*) . . . What kind of deal can you give me?

GROSS
We'll give you the first 40 planes off the assembly line.

JACK
That'll give us about two years exclusivity with her.

HOWARD
More than that. United and American don't have the imagination for a plane like this.

JACK
Two years ahead of Juan Trippe then.

HOWARD considers. Finally turns back to them.

> HOWARD
>
> How much?

> GROSS
>
> 450,000 each.

> HOWARD
>
> 18 million for the first forty . . . Hell, TWA can't afford that. The damn airline is flat broke . . . I guess I'll just have to pay for them myself . . . *(to* **GROSS***)* . . . Build 'em, Bob, and send the bill to Noah Dietrich. Thanks.

He strides out of the hangar quickly.

JACK and **GROSS** look at each other.

In the blink of an eye **HOWARD** has just placed the largest commercial aircraft order in history.

> JACK
>
> Merry Christmas.

INT. MUIRFIELD—DEN. DAY.

HOWARD is on the phone, highly amused:

> HOWARD (ON PHONE)
>
> . . . now don't get all hysterical, Noah, that's not good for you . . . *(smiles)* . . . Yeah, I know it's a lot of money . . . I know, I know, I should have told you but it just slipped my mind . . .

KATE enters. He is surprised to see her.

HOWARD (ON PHONE)

I'll get back to you, thanks . . . *(he hangs up)* . . . Hey, honey, what are you doing home?

KATE

(crisply)
You're not one for tears and neither am I, so best to come out with it directly: I've met someone. I've fallen in love and I'm moving out. If I could make it more gentle I would, but I can't, so there we both are.

HOWARD

(stunned)
What?

KATE

Now let's be honest, this has all been a grand adventure but it couldn't possibly last. We're too alike you and I—

HOWARD

You met someone?

KATE

Someone more appropriate to me, I mean.

HOWARD

What does that mean—"appropriate"?

KATE

Someone more attuned to my needs.

HOWARD

Stop acting, Katie. Look at me.

KATE

I'm not acting.

HOWARD

I wonder if you even know anymore.

KATE

Don't be unkind.

HOWARD

(standing, angry)
Fine—you wanna go—go on. Actresses are cheap in this town, darling, and I have a lot of money.

KATE

This is beneath you—

HOWARD

No, this is exactly me! You come in here out of the blue and tell me you're leaving just like that—and you have the *nerve* to expect graciousness?!

KATE

I expect a little maturity. I expect you to face the situation like an adult who—

HOWARD

Don't talk down to me.

A tense beat.

HOWARD

Don't you ever talk down to me. You're a movie star. Nothing more.

She looks at him. About to crumble. She will never let him see that. She turns and goes.

He stands.

EXT. MUIRFIELD—BACKYARD. NIGHT.

4:00 A.M. **HOWARD** stands at a bonfire raging in the backyard. He is tossing armfuls of clothes into it. Gorgeous suits and shirts and shoes and hats go into the inferno.

He finishes throwing the clothes into the fire. He watches it, the red flame bathing his face.

Then he slowly slips off his jacket. Then shirt. Then everything.

INT. NOAH'S HOUSE—BEDROOM. NIGHT.

NOAH is fast asleep next to his **WIFE**. The phone by the bed rings. Again. **NOAH** opens one eye, looks at the phone.

      NOAH'S WIFE
Don't answer it.

NOAH answers wearily:

      NOAH (ON PHONE)
What is it, Howard?

Split-screen to **HOWARD** at home, he stands nude in his den as the bonfire continues to rage in the backyard.

      HOWARD (ON PHONE)
Hey, Noah, I need you to get over to the Penney's and buy me some new clothes.

      NOAH (ON PHONE)
Penney's isn't open.

      HOWARD (ON PHONE)
Oh, shit. All right, first thing tomorrow. I want two suits off the rack, one light and one dark. Three white shirts.

And three white pairs of tennis shoes. Got that? No, wait, make it Woolworth's. No, no, no, Penney's—*(he stops, suddenly suspicious)*—Noah, do you have a recorder? Are you *recording* this conversation?!

NOAH (ON PHONE)

No . . .

HOWARD (ON PHONE)

Okay, I'm trusting you. Listen, I need those clothes first thing, thanks—Wait! Wait! Wait!—Did I say Penney's or Woolworth's?

NOAH (ON PHONE)

Penney's

HOWARD (ON PHONE)

Better make it Sears.

He hangs up. End *split-screen*.

NOAH hangs up. Sighs.

INT. MUIRFIELD—DEN. NIGHT.

HOWARD stands and watches his clothes burn. We watch his face. Alone. Abandoned.

INT. WAREHOUSE. NIGHT.

Click-click-click . . . The click of high heels on cement.

FAITH DOMERGUE walks across the empty plain of a warehouse floor. The echoing warehouse appears to be vacant but for a single chair with a strong light next to it.

HOWARD sits in the chair, the bright light is focused on FAITH so she cannot really see him.

FAITH is a beautiful brunette. She tries to appear older than her years, feigning a sophistication that is not natural for her.

> HOWARD
> You can stop there, if you please, Miss Domergue.

She stops. Trapped in the glare of the light.

> HOWARD
> Would you take off your heels, please?

She slips out of her shoes. Holds them.

> HOWARD
> Good. Would you turn around, please?

She slowly turns, trying to do it like she saw Rita Hayworth do in a movie once.

> HOWARD
> You know the kind of work it takes to be an actress? It takes hard work. Voice lessons and deportment lessons. And new makeup and wardrobe. It's just like going to school again.

A beat.

> HOWARD
> Would you wipe off your lipstick, please?

She takes a handkerchief from her purse and wipes off her dark red lipstick. It smears a bit.

                         HOWARD
         And the rouge? Could you do something about that, please?

She licks the handkerchief and attempts to clean off the rouge. Does okay.
Without the makeup she is even more attractive. More herself anyway.

                         HOWARD
         Now you understand you'll be under contract to me, person-
         ally. You know what that means? You know what a contract
         is? It's a very serious thing. It's a legal document.

She nods.

A beat.

                         HOWARD
         How old are you, Miss Domergue?

                         FAITH
         15.

A beat.

                         HOWARD
         Holy Mother of God.

INT. COCOANUT GROVE. NIGHT.

We are amidst a sea of elegant shoes effortlessly swaying across a dance
floor. All the shoes are formal, black.

Then a pair of white tennis shoes dances past.

HOWARD is dancing with **FAITH**. He wears his plain dark suit from
Sears. White shirt. White sneakers.

To our surprise, perhaps, **HOWARD** is a very good dancer.

They dance as we go to . . .

A bit later. **HOWARD** and **FAITH** sit in a corner booth with **JACK FRYE** and his wife, **HELEN**.

                    FAITH
(happily)
. . . Car picks me up every morning at eight and off I go. I'm getting my High School diploma. Howard thinks education is important. Then after classes I'm off for elocution and grooming and fittings . . .

                    JACK
(seeing someone)
Well, blow me down . . .

JUAN TRIPPE is approaching the table.

TRIPPE wears a nice suit. Except for a smattering of military uniforms, **TRIPPE** and **HOWARD** are the only men in the entire club not wearing tuxedos. They are worthy adversaries.

TRIPPE arrives at the table.

                    TRIPPE
(shaking hands)
Jack, Helen, hello.

                    JACK
Hello, Juan.

                    TRIPPE
How are you, Howard?

                    HOWARD
(shakes hands)
Good, thanks. This is Miss Domergue.

JACK
Sit down. Now what the hell are you doing out here?

TRIPPE
(pulling a chair to the booth)
Meeting with Douglas on the DC-4, our new plane. She's gonna be a pip . . . *(to **HOWARD**)* . . . How's the Constellation coming?

HOWARD
Good. Great.

TRIPPE
How 'bout letting me steal a peek?

HOWARD
(smiles)
Don't think so.

TRIPPE
You know, I ought to be cross with you. You stole Ray Loewy from us.

HOWARD
He's doing our interior design.

TRIPPE
He was doing ours. What are your colors?

JACK
Stop fishing.

TRIPPE laughs.

HOWARD
Do you have buttons or zippers?

                        TRIPPE

Sorry?

                        HOWARD

On the drapes for the sleeping berths.

                        TRIPPE

Zippers.

                        HOWARD

Oh.

                        TRIPPE

Buttons?

                        HOWARD

Uh-huh.

TRIPPE considers this. **FAITH** is rather mystified at the seriousness of all this.

                        TRIPPE

So I suppose you'll be expanding to Mexico.

                        JACK

Why do you say that?

                        TRIPPE

Your range is 3,000 miles. You'll expand from Los Angeles to Mexico. Maybe South America.

                        JACK

(smiles)
Hey, that's a good idea, anyone got a pen?

                        HOWARD

Or across the Atlantic.

A beat. **JACK** freezes. **TRIPPE** smiles.

> TRIPPE

Too far.

> HOWARD

New York to Newfoundland to Ireland to Paris.

> TRIPPE

Well, Pan Am welcomes you. We're overbooked as it is. It's a great burden having to do it all. When's the Connie coming out?

> HOWARD

Next year maybe. DC-4?

> TRIPPE

Next year.

> HOWARD

I look forward to her.

> TRIPPE

And I to the Connie . . . *(he stands, and delivers a final knife thrust)* . . . I already ordered the next forty after you . . . You know, I never knew you could dance. That was a rhumba, yes?

He smiles and leaves the table. **HOWARD** watches him go.

> JACK

Good going, boss. You just gave him our entire postwar strategy.

> HOWARD

He can't stop us.

JACK

He's Pan Am, Howard. He can stop anything . . . *(hailing passing waiter)* . . . Hey, fella, gimme the biggest scotch you got.

                        HOWARD

Excuse me.

He stands and makes his way through the club, deep in thought. He goes into the men's room . . .

INT. COCOANUT GROVE—MEN'S ROOM. NIGHT.

The bathroom is empty. **HOWARD** moves to a sink, taking his little bar of lye soap from his pocket.

He begins washing his hands. Scrubbing his hands.

He looks into the mirror as he scours his hands. His hands move more quickly now. A certain urgency to the washing. And then almost violence. He does not look down.

His hands are raw now. His face is almost passive as he looks at himself in the mirror.

One of his hands is bleeding now. The lye stings him. He stops, looks down.

A little bit of blood. He stares at it. Surprised.

He quickly rinses off his hands and puts the soap back in his pocket. Dries his hands with a towel, dabbing away the tiny bit of blood.

Then he goes to leave the bathroom. Reaches for the door—

Stops.

He stares at the doorknob.

HOWARD'S POV—EXTREME CLOSEUP—the glistening gold doorknob.

His hands are clean now. He can't touch the doorknob. What to do?

He looks around.

> HOWARD
> Hello . . . ?

No one else is in the bathroom.

He looks at the doorknob again. Frustrated.

Then an idea. He shifts his position. Ready. He waits.

Then a man sweeps into the bathroom. **HOWARD** nips out the open door.

INT. COCOANUT GROVE. NIGHT.

HOWARD returns to the table, all business:

> HOWARD
> All right, I want you to get in touch with Mr. Joyce and Mr. Berg. They're my boys in Washington. And set up a meeting with Jesse Jones, he's Secretary of Commerce, old golfing buddy—

> JACK
> Whoa, slow down—

> HOWARD
> We're gonna need terminals in Ireland and France and I want some tax breaks from them. If that bastard thinks he

owns the whole goddamn world he's got another think coming.

JACK
Pan Am owns Europe. But he's smart, we ought to think about Mexico.

HOWARD
(very firm)
To hell with Mexico. No one airline should have a *monopoly* on flying the Atlantic. That's just not fair!

HOWARD leans in. We have rarely seen him this intense.

HOWARD
He owns Pan Am. He owns Congress. He owns the Civil Aeronautics Board. *But he does not own the sky.*

HOWARD notes his hand is bleeding again. Just a spot of blood. He presses it to his pant leg to stop the bleeding.

HOWARD
We're in a street fight with that sonofabitch and I am not going to lose. I been fighting high hat, Ivy League pricks like him my whole life. And listen, fire Ray Loewy. He's spying for Trippe. That shitheel knew all about the buttons. Spies in my midst. 'Scuse me.

And **HOWARD** is up and gone, heading toward the bathroom again.

INT. MUIRFIELD—DEN. NIGHT.

HOWARD sits at his desk, slowly flipping through a series of grainy black-and-white photos, shot through a telephoto lens. Surveillance photos.

The photos show **KATE** with **SPENCER TRACY**. They are on a boat. The photos range from cozily domestic to romantic to erotic.

A large man sits across from **HOWARD**. He is a brooding Cuban man called **JORGE**, Howard's chief private investigator and enforcer. A sinister presence more than a man, **JORGE** takes care of all the ugly little details.

HOWARD completes flipping through the photos. Shuts his eyes. A long beat.

> HOWARD
>
> Where did you get them?

> JORGE
>
> From their photo lab. One of the technicians.

HOWARD opens his eyes. Cold, resolute fury.

EXT. SAN PEDRO PARK. NIGHT.

Dead of night. A car slowly pulls up to an isolated park overlooking the ocean. The car's headlights find **HOWARD** and **JORGE** standing at a fence, beyond the fence is a sheer drop to the roaring ocean below.

ROLAND SWEET, the editor of HOLLYWOOD EXPOSE magazine, climbs from the car. He leaves the headlights on, illuminating the scene.

SWEET goes to them, offering his hand.

> SWEET
>
> Hello, Howard.

> HOWARD
> *(not shaking)*
> Roland.

SWEET glances to the brooding **JORGE**. No introduction is made.

                            SWEET
So what can I do for you?

                            HOWARD
I want the pictures you have of Kate Hepburn and Spencer Tracy. All the negatives. And I want you to kill the story.

                            SWEET
Sorry, we're set to run next month.

                            HOWARD
I would take it as a personal favor if you wouldn't do that.

                            SWEET
He's a married man and he's a Catholic and they're both movie stars. Fair game all around.

HOWARD gazes at him. Doesn't say anything. **HOWARD**'s cool eyes burn into **SWEET**. The silence grows. Ominous. **SWEET** glances to **JORGE**. The ocean roars below.

                            SWEET
My office knows where I am, Howard.

                            HOWARD
I'm not going to kill you, Roland. I don't do that.

A beat.

                            HOWARD
How much?

                            SWEET
Not for sale.

                            HOWARD
How much?

SWEET
Not. For. Sale.

A beat. **JORGE** puts his hands into his coat pockets.

HOWARD
You ever cheat on your wife, Roland? . . . You ever screw a colored girl? . . . You ever steal anything? . . . You ever hurt anyone?

A beat.

HOWARD
You ever go to a Communist party meeting, Roland?

SWEET blinks. A beat.

SWEET
TWA stock.

HOWARD
How much?

SWEET
50,000 shares.

HOWARD
10.

SWEET
All right.

HOWARD turns without a word and strides off, **JORGE** with him.

SWEET remains frozen in the lights of his car. As we hear:

> HOWARD (V.O.)
> What do you think about Trans *World* Airways . . . ?

Taking us to . . .

INT. AVA'S MANSION—BEDROOM. EVENING.

White orchids fill a luxurious bedroom.

A woman is bent over, brushing her long, raven hair. We do not see her face. Then she stands, tossing her head back, shaking her hair loose.

And we see her face. **AVA GARDNER**. The one and only.

HOWARD sits across from her, feet up.

> HOWARD
> . . . Transcontinental and Western just doesn't fit anymore. Now that we're going international we need a name that reflects that.

> AVA
> Trans World is good. Kinda peppy.

> HOWARD
> TWA. Keep the same initials. That way we don't have to repaint the planes.

> AVA
> That's you, always pinching pennies . . . Hand me my wrap.

He fetches her fur stole. Drapes it around her shoulders. Being this close is too much. The scent of her. The allure. He kisses her shoulders. Inhaling her.

She wriggles away.

                              AVA

Knock it off.

                            HOWARD

I have something for you.

He gets a white cardboard box. Hands it to her. She is displeased.

                              AVA

What the hell is this?

                            HOWARD

It's a present. Open it up.

She opens the box. Inside is shredded newspaper.

                              AVA

Oh. A box of trash. You shouldn't have.

                            HOWARD

Keep looking.

She frowns and sorts through the newspaper. Feels something. She pulls out a necklace. A stunning necklace of diamonds and one gigantic sapphire. It is breathtaking.

                            HOWARD
                            (*eager*)
It's a Kashmiri sapphire, best in the world. I had my boys all over the damn globe looking for this.

                              AVA

Why?

                            HOWARD

Because it matches your eyes.

She drops the necklace back into the box, hands it to him.

                    AVA

I'm not for sale.

                    HOWARD

For Christ sake, it's just a present—

                    AVA

(a flash of her famed anger)
You can't buy me, so stop trying. Don't buy me anymore diamonds or sapphires or any other goddamn thing. You can buy me dinner. How about that?

                    HOWARD

Jesus, Ava—

                    AVA

How much are you willing to spend? What does a human being cost, Howard?

                    HOWARD

20,000 dollars.

She stops. Looks at him.

                    AVA

What?

                    HOWARD

A human being costs 20,000 dollars. Well, it might be more now.

                    AVA

What . . . are . . . you . . . talking . . . about?

                        HOWARD
A few years ago I was driving down Third. This man stepped into the street. Or maybe I wasn't paying attention. I killed him with the car. It cost me 20,000 dollars to settle with his family. As I say, it might be more now.

He stands there. Like a lost little boy.

INT. CHEVY. EVENING.

HOWARD is cruising with **AVA** in one of his hideous Chevys. She is dressed to kill, her mink stole around her shoulders.

                        AVA
. . . It's bad enough I have to endure those filthy gym shoes of yours, but then I get all dolled up and we have to go out in this old jalopy without a hood!

                        HOWARD
Hey, Ava, will you marry me?

                        AVA
No, Howard.

                        HOWARD
Why not?

                        AVA
In the first place, I don't love you. In the second place, I'm still married . . . Look, you got girls stashed all over town—you got a damned harem just at the Bel Air—why don't you marry one of your bungalow girls?

                        HOWARD
Those are *employees*. I can't marry an employee, how would that look?

Suddenly a car SLAMS into them—into the passenger door—**HOWARD** and **AVA** rock, not really injured, the Chevy stops—then the car that hit them backs up and drives into them again—SLAM—and again—SLAM.

HOWARD leaps out—

EXT. STREET. FOLLOWING.

FAITH is plowing into them, demolishing the front of her sporty roadster. Demolishing the Chevy's passenger door.

HOWARD runs toward her—

> HOWARD
> Faith! What the hell—?!

He jumps back as **FAITH** plows into the Chevy one last time. She attempts to back up again but her roadster dies, steam hissing from the engine.

> HOWARD
> Goddammit—what the hell is this?!

> FAITH
> *(dissolving)*
> What are you doing with her?

> HOWARD
> We're going to dinner, now get out of there—

> FAITH
> *(wailing, a teenager)*
> Don't you love me anymore—?

> HOWARD
> 'Course I do, little baby, you just have to—

FAITH bawls.

Meanwhile, **AVA** is screaming through her window:

AVA
GET THAT CRAZY CUNT AWAY FROM ME!

FAITH continues to wail. **AVA** continues to scream.

A crowd is beginning to form. Someone flashes a picture. **HOWARD** tries to shield his face. Too late—

QUICK FLASHES: A series of ugly black and white shots of the crash— **HOWARD** shielding his face—**AVA** screaming—**HOWARD** awkwardly trying to get **FAITH** out of her car—**HOWARD** angry at the photographer—

The final photo burns into a tabloid cover . . .

INT. JUAN TRIPPE'S OFFICE—PAN AM. DAY.

. . . The tabloid cover sits on **JUAN TRIPPE**'s desk. **TRIPPE** sits across from an imposing older man.

He is **SENATOR RALPH OWEN BREWSTER**, a cagey politician with an easy and smooth manner. A smiling carnivore.

Title: Senator Ralph Owen Brewster. Republican. Maine.

BREWSTER
. . . and Jack Frye's been lobbying everyone in town. He's got the British and French ambassadors on board now . . . TWA's serious about going international.

TRIPPE slowly taps his pipe clean.

TRIPPE
Point, Mr. Hughes.

A beat. **TRIPPE** is thinking ten moves in advance.

TRIPPE
Very well, I think it's time you introduced the Community Airline Bill in the Senate.

BREWSTER
Is it done?

TRIPPE
My people are finishing it now. And I'll need you on the Committee Investigating the National Defense.

BREWSTER
On the Committee? . . . Or Chairman? . . . Harry Truman was Chairman of that Committee and look what it did for him. It's a great public platform, always generates a lot of press.

TRIPPE looks at him. Nods.

TRIPPE
Chairman it is . . . (he gets some airplane blueprints) . . . Now let me show you the D-C 4 . . .

INT. HUGHES AIRCRAFT—HERCULES HANGAR. NIGHT.

HOWARD walks through a fair representation of Hell. The Hercules hangar.

The harsh blue glare of acetylene torches and welding irons send horrifying shadows into the upper reaches of the chamber. The thunk and groan of heavy machinery echo like tourists' calls into the Grand Canyon. The hangar is 800 feet long.

Hundreds of workers labor in every corner of the massive hangar. Most of them swarming over ...

The skeletal frame of the Hercules' fuselage. The combination of wood and plastic molding soars up, disappearing into the darkness at the top of the cathedral.

HOWARD is particularly intense—*in overdrive*—his mind racing, battling to keep up with the many, many pressures of his life. He flips through renderings for a new TWA logo as he walks, tossing aside those he doesn't like—which is all of them.

An **AIDE** scurries behind and picks up the discarded renderings.

JACK FRYE strides alongside **HOWARD**.

> JACK
> ... If the Community Airline Bill becomes law we are finished, my friend. Pan Am will have a legal monopoly on international travel and—

> HOWARD
> How can they justify it? It's un-American.

> JACK
> Senator Brewster is saying that domestic competition will kill expansion into the global market—because the nationalized foreign carriers, like Air France and Lufthansa, can offer lower fares 'cause they don't have to *compete*, right? So, hey, let's get rid of all that messy competition and have a *nationalized* airline of our own. And, hey, why don't we make it Pan Am?

A very overtired **GLENN ODEKIRK** calls down to **HOWARD** from the top of a step unit alongside the plane:

> GLENN
> Howard, I need you up here.

HOWARD turns to the **AIDE** collecting up the TWA logo renderings:

> HOWARD
> We're Trans *World* Airways—give me a goddamn globe or a circle or something *round* for Christ sake!

HOWARD climbs up the step unit toward **GLENN** as he continues to **JACK** with singular intensity:

> HOWARD
> All right, we gotta go public with this. I'll talk to Hearst and see what kinda press he can give me. But sooner or later it's gonna come down to a vote in the Senate. So we gotta get some Senators on our side—see who's up for reelection and start making campaign contributions—

> JACK
> You want me to bribe Senators?

> HOWARD
> I don't want 'em bribed, I want 'em *bought*. And put a team of investigators on Senator Brewster. I need to know everything there is about that shitbag. Where he goes, what he says, and who he screws. Get into it. *Right now, Jack.*

> JACK
> You got it.

JACK returns down the step unit.

HOWARD joins **GLENN** at the top of the steps and they enter . . .

INT. HERCULES HANGAR—FUSELAGE. DAY.

. . . The great, yawning chasm that is the hollow interior of the Hercules' fuselage under construction. Truly the belly of the beast.

GLENN leads HOWARD to a collection of huge blueprints.

                        HOWARD
What do you need?

                        GLENN
Left rear rudder and elevators.

HOWARD studies some blueprints, the bustling fuselage stretching out beyond him, seemingly forever, like a nightmare vision from a Bosch painting.

HOWARD makes some quick notes on the blueprints and then proceeds out of the fuselage as:

                        HOWARD
Those others are fine but have Simon and Pete get back to me on the power coupling relays, we need redundant systems here... And listen, we gotta take another look at the wheel—

                        GLENN
Oh Jesus—the damn wheel—

                        HOWARD
It doesn't feel right.

INT. HERCULES HANGAR. NIGHT.

Back down on the hangar floor, HOWARD and GLENN are at a mammoth collection of prototype steering wheels for the Hercules. Every conceivable shape and size and material.

HOWARD patiently tries them out as GLENN melts down:

                        GLENN
Howard, we've tried every goddamn thing—we've tried

leather, we've tried plastic, we've tried metal, with ridges, round, flat, square—Christ almighty you have seen eight thousand goddamn wheels—you gotta make a decision!

                      HOWARD
(trying out a wheel)
I don't know, this one's pretty close . . .

HOWARD stops, watching a **CUSTODIAN** sweeping up. Little dust tornadoes around his broom. The **CUSTODIAN** is looking at **HOWARD** evenly. It's a bit sinister.

HOWARD'S POV—EXTREME CLOSEUP—the dust tornadoes swirling into the air—the **CUSTODIAN**'s steady gaze—the broom sending up more and more dust particles—

HOWARD tears himself back to reality:

                      HOWARD
That man sweeping up. Does he work for me? I mean, have you seen him before?

                      GLENN
Name's Josh or something like that.

                      HOWARD
Why is he looking at me?

                      GLENN
I don't know.

HOWARD turns back to the wheels, continues trying various ones.

                      HOWARD
Fire him. And make sure they use damp brooms from now on. Respiratory diseases are expensive and I don't want a bunch of damn lawsuits . . .

GLENN

Okay. But can we at least proceed with the instrument panel we discussed? The tool shop is ready to go—

HOWARD

No, I wanna see the blueprints again—

GLENN

(cracking a bit)
You've seen all this stuff a hundred times—it's just like the damn wheel—you can't keep changing your mind—we're eight goddamn months behind schedule as it is–!

HOWARD

It's all gotta be right—it's got to *feel* right.

GLENN

Look, you gotta face it, the deadline is now totally unrealistic. At this rate the war will be over by the time she's done!

HOWARD

(calming)
Odie, take it easy . . . I understand you're under a lot of pressure, but it's gonna do me no good if you crack up on me. Take a couple hours off . . .

His eyes dart to the **CUSTODIAN** again. The same even gaze at **HOWARD**.

HOWARD

. . . Relax a little bit, take some time off. See your wife. Just be sure to show me all the blueprints. Show me all the blueprints. Show me all the blueprints. Show me all the blueprints . . .

GLENN looks at him. A half smile. Is this a joke?

                            HOWARD
    . . . Show me all the blueprints. Show me all the blueprints.
    Show me all the blueprints . . .

HOWARD's face. A terrible flash of fear in his eyes.

It has finally happened. He is going mad.

And he knows it. He can't stop himself.

                            HOWARD
    . . . Show me all the blueprints. Show me all the blueprints.
    Show me all the blueprints . . .

                            GLENN
    (concerned)
    Howard . . . ?

HOWARD's face. Incredible fear. He knows what's happening and he just can't stop it.

                            HOWARD
    . . . Show me all the blueprints. Show me all the blueprints.
    Show me all the blueprints . . .

HOWARD, still repeating neurotically, backs away from **GLENN** and hurries out of the hangar.

INT. HOWARD'S CAR—HUGHES AIRCRAFT. NIGHT.

HOWARD sits in his car, his hands clamped over his mouth.

He refuses to remove them, terrified of what might come out. We see the panic in his eyes. Finally he closes his eyes and prepares himself. He slowly removes his hands.

Silence. He opens his eyes and dares to speak:

>HOWARD
>Quarantine. Q-U-A-R-A-N-T-I-N-E. Quarantine.

He has done it.

Not mad. Not yet.

EXT. HUGHES AIRCRAFT-RUNWAY DAY

The XF-11. At last.

It is the first time we have see the great plane outdoors. It is the first time anyone has seen her outdoors. Her inaugural flight.

Like a great panther waiting to pounce, she sits on the endless runway. We can feel her coiled muscles, her power. Her unique twin rear booms soar out behind her with feline grace, like a sleek Art Deco hood ornament.

HOWARD once called her "the most beautiful plane ever built." He was not wrong.

Title: July 7, 1946. Inaugural flight of the XF-11.

INT./EXT. XF-11. DAY.

HOWARD, wearing his lucky fedora, is settling into the cockpit. Built for military reconnaissance, the cockpit is incredibly complicated; a womb of gauges and dials and switches and levers and weapon controls and camera relays.

HOWARD gazes at the chaos of controls as he fastens his safety harness across his chest.

Meanwhile, **GLENN** is at the Command Post at the side of the runway. An army of technicians and engineers await. **PROFESSOR FITZ** as well, monitoring a weather radar console. **GLENN** settles in behind a radio set, puts on his headset.

A delegation of Air Force officers is there as well, checking on their investment.

Inside the XF-11, **HOWARD** activates his radio:

HOWARD
Odie, you reading me okay?

GLENN (V.O. ON RADIO)
Yeah, Howard, you're a-okay.

HOWARD
Starting ignition sequence.

He throws a series of toggles and presses ignition. The engines begin to hum. The propellers begin to spin. He watches them through the plexiglass bubble dome of the cockpit.

He takes the wheel gently, manipulates the plane's controls, efficiently preparing the plane.

GLENN (V.O. ON RADIO)
Okay, Howard, confirm visual action. She's all yours.

HOWARD gently caresses the foot pedals, hand levers and wheel.

Outside, the mighty XF-11 begins to roll.

Inside, smooth as silk. Stasis and calm as the world slowly rolls by outside.

                           HOWARD
She's goddamn spotless, Odie! No wiggle on the wheel or
throttles.

                     GLENN (V.O. ON RADIO)
Take it easy, Howard . . .

                           HOWARD
Preparing for starboard turn 1-8-0.

He elegantly swings the plane around. Clean. The long runway stretches
out before him.

                     GLENN (V.O. ON RADIO)
How does she sound, Howard?

                           HOWARD
She's whispering to me, buddy.

                     GLENN (V.O. ON RADIO)
All right. Make her sing.

HOWARD smiles and sets the plane in motion. She begins to zoom
down the runway, gaining momentum.

She ROARS past Glenn and the others at the Command Post.

The XF-11 gracefully soars into the sky.

Inside, silk.

HOWARD laughs.

                           HOWARD
Well, Odie, she can fly, congratulations.

GLENN (V.O. ON RADIO)

Retract landing gear and climb to 5,000 feet at a heading of due West 4-5.

HOWARD

Retracting landing gear and climbing to 5,000 feet at a heading of due West 4-5.

He switches the landing gear lever and climbs.

All of a sudden he is over the Pacific Ocean. In the blink of an eye the world has been left behind.

HOWARD

Jesus, she's fast!

GLENN (V.O. ON RADIO)

What's your airspeed, Howard?

HOWARD

2-9-2.

GLENN (V.O. ON RADIO)

Take her back to 2-0-0.

HOWARD

No . . . goddamn . . . way.

He pulls back on the wheel and the XF-11 streaks through the sky.

And is lost in the clouds.

An eternal moment as **HOWARD** soars. His dream. The world behind him, the heavens before him. Airborne. Clean. Free.

The glorious XF-11 responds to his every tiny cue, melting to his commands like butter. The insane power of the H-1 has been replaced with a serene clam.

An hour and forty-five minutes later . . .

INT./EXT. XF-11. DAY.

HOWARD is soaring over Los Angeles at 5,000 feet. Bliss.

> GLENN (V.O. ON RADIO)
> Howard, we gotta bring her home. Set course for port turn 1-8-0 and return to base. Descend to 4,000 feet.

> HOWARD
> Gimme ten more minutes.

> GLENN (V.O. ON RADIO)
> Negative, Howard. Bring her home.

> HOWARD
> Okay, setting course for—

And then it happens.

The plane SLAMS to the right. Dipping savagely. As if a giant were pulling it back and down by the right wing.

> HOWARD
> Christ—!

> GLENN (V.O. ON RADIO)
> *(alert)*
> What is it, Howard?

> HOWARD
> The right wing just dipped—Jesus Christ—(he fights with the controls)—I'm losing starboard engine.

The XF-11 begins to list dangerously to the right, losing altitude.

> HOWARD
> Increasing power to 2,800 rpm—(no good)—cutting back—increasing starboard engine power only—(no good)—cutting back. I'm losing altitude.

> GLENN (V.O. ON RADIO)
> Check starboard engine indicator.

> HOWARD
> *(confused)*
> Lights are green.

The XF-11 continues to soar down, tilting to the right.

> GLENN (V.O. ON RADIO)
> Are both starboard props turning?

> HOWARD
> Hold on.

He quickly releases his safety harness, stands forward in the listing cockpit to see—the plane swerves to the right—**HOWARD** scrambles to hold on—fighting with the wheel—sits back down.

Does not refasten his harness.

> HOWARD
> Looks like they are, Odie—but she's pulling me back and starboard.

> GLENN (V.O. ON RADIO)
> *(calming)*
> Howard, return to base. Repeat, return to base.

The XF-11 is losing altitude quickly. Soaring toward the ground. The altimeter arrow floats down past 3,500 feet . . . 3,000 feet . . .

HOWARD jams his feet on the pedals, fights with the wheel.

> HOWARD
> I'm at full left rudder and full left aileron but she won't stay level—

The altimeter: 2,500 feet . . . 2,000 feet . . .

> GLENN (V.O. ON RADIO)
> Howard, give us your position.

> HOWARD
> 2,000 feet over—Christ, I dunno, Beverly Hills—1,500 feet.

> GLENN (V.O. ON RADIO)
> Reduce engines to 1,000.

> HOWARD
> We're going down—I'm gonna try for the Wilshire Country Club ninth hole. Oughta be wide enough. You read me, Odie?

> GLENN (V.O. ON RADIO)
> Wilshire Country Club. Reduce engines to 1,000.

The plane is zooming toward the earth. The quiet residential streets of Beverly Hills flying up at **HOWARD**. Impossibly fast—

The G-forces of the fall are now pressing **HOWARD** back into his seat—

Beverly Hills zooms up—

With every ounce of strength in him, **HOWARD** fights to keep the nose of the plane up—

Then he sees it is too late—

HOWARD
I'm not going to make it, buddy.

The houses of Beverly Hills are zooming up at him—

At the very last moment he prepares himself for impact by throwing himself back and thrusting his feet forward—slamming them onto the panels ahead of him as—

The XF-11 crashes.

The Most Beautiful Plane In The World slashes through a roof, slicing it off like a cake—

HOWARD's whole body snaps forward—

The right wing smashes into a corner of another house, exploding and tearing through a second floor bedroom in a ball of flame—

HOWARD's face smashes into the plexiglass cockpit dome, shards of plexiglass and metal slicing into him—

The remainder of the right wing tears through the corner of another house, demolishing it, and suddenly sending the plane on a ferocious roll, end-over-end—

HOWARD slams around the demolished cockpit—

The plane bounces and rolls—severing a utility pole—crashing through an alley—

HOWARD is thrown violently around the cockpit, slamming from control panel to seat to plexiglass dome—

The plane disintegrates into four flaming sections as it tears through the alley—

Flames explode around **HOWARD** in the fuselage—

The fuselage finally SLAMS to a stop in the alley—

HOWARD careens forward, his body grotesquely mangled—

But conscious.

Blood pours from his face—

The fuselage around him is quickly filling with noxious black smoke—Howard hacks violently for breath—

He looks around desperately. He has to get out, away from the killing smoke—

He sees the plexiglass cockpit dome and tries to pull himself toward it—but his left foot is trapped in a chaos of twisting metal—

Still fighting for air in the smoky fuselage, he pulls at his trapped left leg—finally wrenches his leg free—shattering his left ankle—he claws and hauls himself up to the cockpit dome—

His eyes are blood red and stinging. His lungs are burning, every breath of the acrid smoke is agony—

For leverage he must grab onto the boiling rubber rim of the cockpit bubble—he does, searing both hands to the bone—he hauls himself up—shoving at the bubble with his shoulders—it finally gives way—

WHOOSH—the sudden rush of air from outside creates a hellish backdraft—a burst of FLAME shoots quickly over him—

He tries to pull himself from the cockpit—his left hand catches fire—he furiously tries to extinguish it by beating it on the sleeve of his jacket—

His jacket catches on fire—

In desperation he throws himself from the cockpit and falls to the wing—through the flames—

He rolls off the wing and falls to the ground—furiously trying to drag himself free—

Then can do nothing more. He collapses. It's over.

He lies there as the flames consume him—his eyes open—aware of everything—

Then a vision through the acrid black smoke and flames—

A man racing down the alley toward him, a **MARINE**.

The brave **MARINE** fights through the flames and grabs **HOWARD**—yanks him from the burning wreckage—

Pulls him away from the plane—

>MARINE
>IS THERE ANYONE ELSE INSIDE?!

HOWARD can't hear—

>MARINE
>IS THERE ANYONE ELSE?!

HOWARD shakes his head and then grabs the **MARINE**'s collar, pulls himself forward toward the man's face until he is inches away—

HOWARD's face is mangled; a bloody, shredded mass of scorched tissue and bone.

With his last breath he gurgles through the blood streaming from his mouth:

> HOWARD
> I'm Howard Hughes. The aviator.

Then—

A **PHOTOGRAPHER** appears and flashes a picture—FOOSH—**HOWARD** writhes in agony, screaming—

He is captured in the harsh white explosion of the flashbulb. Dying.

INT. HOSPITAL CORRIDOR. NIGHT.

There has never been a death watch like this one.

The corridor outside **HOWARD**'s room is filled. **JACK FRYE** sits with his head down. **ERROL FLYNN** leans against a wall, chatting with **JOHNNY MEYER**. **GLENN ODEKIRK** sits with several of his engineers, furiously arguing over XF-11 blueprints. **AVA** sits, wearing dark glasses, pretending to read a magazine.

NOAH is standing in a secluded corner with a **DOCTOR**:

> DOCTOR
> . . . He has burns on 78 percent of his body. Nine ribs are shattered—not broken, shattered—as are his nose, cheek, chin, left knee and left elbow. He has 60 lacerations on his face to the bone. His chest was crushed so his left lung has collapsed and his heart has shifted entirely to the right side of his chest cavity.

                             NOAH

Jesus God . . .

                            DOCTOR

He's getting blood transfusions now but . . .

                             NOAH

Whose blood?

                            DOCTOR

From our stock.

                             NOAH

Oh, he's not going to like that.

The **DOCTOR** stares at **NOAH**.

                            DOCTOR

Mr. Dietrich, I doubt he's ever going to like or dislike anything again. I'm terribly sorry.

The **DOCTOR** moves away.

NOAH stands for a moment and then goes to **HOWARD**'s door. Takes a breath. Enters . . .

INT. HOSPITAL—HOWARD'S ROOM. FOLLOWING.

NOAH stands and looks at the shattered body of what was once **HOWARD HUGHES**.

HOWARD lies in a coma inside an oxygen tent, connected to chugging machines. He has been bandaged but the bloody horror is evident. A whisper of life is all that remains.

NOAH sinks into a chair, looks at him.

Then we hear:

> HOWARD (V.O.)
> Orange juice . . .

INT. HOSPITAL—HOWARD'S ROOM. DAY.

HOWARD is sitting up in bed. Very weak. His face is almost completely covered in bandages. Only his bloodshot right eye and a bit of his torn, swollen mouth are visible through the shrouding.

NOAH and **GLENN** sit with him.

HOWARD does not move a muscle because of the burns. His collapsed lung makes it difficult to draw breath. He is heavily sedated, almost incoherent.

> HOWARD
> . . . not fresh from the kitchen . . .

A **CHEF** stands in a corner of the room preparing orange juice for **HOWARD**, slicing oranges and squeezing them.

> HOWARD
> Make 'em squeeze it here . . . so I can see . . .

We note that even in his weakened state, **HOWARD**'s voice is strangely louder now. His flat, Texan deaf-man's twang more pronounced. The accident has destroyed his already flawed hearing.

> HOWARD
> . . . Orange juice has . . . nutritional value . . . Flies outside the window, though . . . everyone likes citrus . . . don't they just?

His bloodshot eye settles on **GLENN**:

                    HOWARD
Tell me.

                    GLENN
An oil seal ripped off the starboard propeller. When the pressure dropped, the prop reversed pitch. Do you understand me? . . . *(HOWARD nods)* . . . I hate to bother you now, but there's something else. You following me? . . . *(HOWARD nods)* . . . The Air Force canceled the contract on the Hercules.

This is a body blow. **HOWARD** takes it almost without shuddering.

                    GLENN
The war's been over for a year. They say they don't need it anymore. I have to know what you want me to do? Should I release the staff?

                    HOWARD
How far . . . from finishing?

                    GLENN
About six months.

                    HOWARD
No . . . in money.

                    GLENN
7 million. Maybe more.

A beat.

                    HOWARD
Build it.

GLENN and **NOAH** exchange a glance.

                                  NOAH
(gently)
Howard, there's something else . . . A Constellation crashed in
Reading, Pennsylvania. Civil Aeronautics Board grounded the
whole fleet.

HOWARD stares at him. Then turns his gaze to a single vase of flowers
in the room.

                                 HOWARD
Juan Trippe sent me flowers.

                                  NOAH
Where are all the others?

                                 HOWARD
Had them taken out . . . They attract aphids . . . Aphids are
awful things . . . But I wanted to see these ones every day.

The chef brings a glass of orange juice to **HOWARD**'s mouth, carefully
inserting the straw through the hole in the bandages by his lips.
HOWARD sucks the straw as he glares at the flowers.

EXT. LOS ANGELES AIRPORT. DAY.

The magnificent Constellations are everything we have waited for. Sleek
and aerodynamic and enormous.

And grounded.

HOWARD slowly limps with **NOAH** and **JACK FRYE** past a fleet of
the idle planes. Bold red-and-white TWA colors on the Connies.

HOWARD is a skeleton. He has lost 35 pounds off his already lean frame.
He is weak, walking with a cane, trying to focus.

It is soon apparent that his face will never be what it was. Plastic surgery has helped, but he has lost much of the natural elasticity on the left side of his face. His amazingly pure beauty is just gone, although a darker, more saturnine intensity gives his face a commanding aspect.

He now sports a mustache to cover a scar above his lip.

HOWARD
How long can they keep us grounded?

JACK
Until they finish their investigation of the Reading crash. That could be months.

NOAH
(to **JACK***)*
Jesus—you're already running a 14 million dollar deficit. How you gonna afford to have them out of service a week much less—?

HOWARD
When we go international, we'll make it up.

NOAH
Look, Brewster's C.A.B. bill just isn't going away. That bill passes and you've bought all these goddamn planes for nothing!

JACK
We're fighting the C.A.B. bill—

NOAH
(ignoring him, to **HOWARD***)*
Meanwhile, how do you suggest we keep TWA flying? And don't just tell me to go to Toolco, we're still pumping every damn cent we have into the Hercules, which, I might add, the Air Force doesn't even want anymore . . .

HOWARD'S POV—EXTREME CLOSEUP—NOAH talking—his words can barely be heard through the now ringing and whooshing torrent of white noise inside Howard's head.

HOWARD turns his good ear to NOAH. It doesn't help much anymore. He forces himself to concentrate.

>   NOAH
> ... it all comes down to this: *you gotta choose*. Do you want to be bankrupt by the big plane or by the big airline?

HOWARD seems about to implode. It is all too much right now. Then he takes several deep breaths. Fights for control.

A long beat as he looks at the Constellations. Then:

>   HOWARD
> Go see Thomas Parkinson at the Equitable in New York. Get a loan against all the TWA equipment and capital. Use the planes as collateral. Hell, use the desks, and the pens and every damn thing we got. Try to get me 40 million.

>   NOAH
> And if TWA defaults on the loan?

>   HOWARD
> Then Juan Trippe buys us cheap.

INT. AVA'S MANSION—LIVING ROOM. DAY.

AVA is raging. And few human beings can rage like AVA GARDNER.

HOWARD, still standing unsteadily with his cane, watches as she stalks dangerously around her living room—brandishing a small covert microphone and wires she has ripped from a wall—

                           AVA

UNDER MY BED?!—YOU PUT A GODDAMN MICRO-
PHONE UNDER MY BED—?!

                         HOWARD

Honey, listen to me—I'm concerned about you, baby, I just
wanna make sure you're okay—

She goes to a window, tears open the drapes—

                           AVA

And who's in that car?! That goddamn car is with me twenty-
four hours a day—

                         HOWARD

It's there for your protection!

                           AVA

The only one I need protected from is *you*, you sick bastard!—
You don't own me, Howard, I'm not one of your teenage
whores and I'm not some damn airplane—!

                         HOWARD

(implores)
Look, I'm sorry, Ava, listen to me, I'll have them take all the
bugs out. You just have to understand that . . . that I need to
know where you are.

                           AVA

Why?

                         HOWARD

Because I worry about you.

                           AVA

Bullshit . . . *(she stops)* . . . What do you mean *all* the bugs?

A beat.

				AVA

What do you mean *all* the bugs?

				HOWARD

There's more.

				AVA

How many?

				HOWARD

Maybe . . . twelve. And on the telephones.

She looks at him. Shocked and saddened in equal measure.

				AVA

Christ, Howard, on the telephone . . . You listen to my phone calls?

				HOWARD

Oh no, honey . . . I just read the transcripts.

A beat as she looks at him, her fury building.

				AVA

What do you wanna know, Howard? Was I screwing Artie Shaw last night, yeah I was. Was I screwing Sinatra the night before, you bet—

				HOWARD

Ava, don't—

She moves in on him relentlessly:

                              AVA
Everyone told me you were a goddamn *lunatic* but I didn't listen. Well, baby, when they finally throw you into the nuthouse—*which they will*—when they're shaving your head for the electroshock, don't come running to me. It's no goddamn wonder Kate Hepburn dumped your demented ass—

He suddenly SHOVES her—hard-

She falls into a chair—instantly recoils and grabs a large marble ashtray—swings it at him savagely—it SLAMS into his forehead.

He stands before her, lost. Blood trickling down his forehead.

She stands, panting.

                              AVA.
Get out of here . . . You pathetic freak.

HOWARD goes.

EXT. AVA'S MANSION. DAY.

HOWARD walks to his car, mumbling to himself, dabbing at the blood on his head with a handkerchief.

JORGE, his Cuban enforcer, is waiting.

                            HOWARD
Take out all the bugs . . . except for the one on the bedroom phone.

                            JORGE
We got a problem at the house.

INT. MUIRFIELD-DEN. DAY.

And the assault begins. Increasing pressure on **HOWARD**.

He stands, extremely tense, on the verge of trauma. His den is being invaded. Total blitzkrieg as his inner sanctum is defiled.

A dozen **FBI AGENTS** and **SENATE INVESTIGATORS** are rifling through his files. He watches as the agents touch his belongings and move things out of the way. One sits at his desk. They are taking pictures of everything.

INT. 7000 ROMAINE—ACCOUNTING OFFICES. DAY.

FBI agents and investigators are sorting through documents at 7000 Romaine and taking pictures. Accountants and secretaries stand about nervously.

NOAH enters quickly.

                    NOAH
What the hell is this?

                    FBI AGENT
(handing him a warrant)
Federal warrant.

EXT. MUIRFIELD. DAY.

HOWARD watches through a window as more agents sort through his garbage. They haul things away and flash photos—

INT. MUIRFIELD. NIGHT.

HOWARD is on a hall phone, his eyes never leaving a new team of agents tearing through his den and flashing photos of everything. **HOWARD** grows increasingly upset.

> HOWARD (ON PHONE, tense)
> ... This is the tenth goddamn time they've been here!—Noah, you gotta help—they are *touching* things, you know what that means?!

HOWARD'S POV—EXTREME CLOSEUP—the FBI agents touching his things—their fingerprints—their shoes trampling across the floor—one agent is smoking, an ash falls to the carpet—

HOWARD just can't bear watching the invasion a moment longer. He drops the phone and hurries away.

The phone hangs at the end of the cord.

> NOAH (V.O. ON PHONE)
> Howard . . . ? Howard . . . ?

INT. MAYFLOWER HOTEL—BREWSTER'S APARTMENT. DAY.

SENATOR BREWSTER is standing, looking over a table set for an elegant lunch for two in his palatial Washington apartment.

Title: February 12, 1947. Mayflower Hotel, Washington DC.

BREWSTER considers the settings for a moment. Then reaches forward and picks up one of the empty water glasses. Puts a thumb print on it. Clearly visible as he holds it to the light. Smiles. Sets the water glass down.

A buzz from the front door.

BREWSTER walks through the apartment, meets **HOWARD** being escorted in by a **MAID**. **HOWARD** wears his dark suit. White shirt. No tie. White sneakers.

HOWARD is making a superhuman effort to appear "normal."

								BREWSTER
Howard, hello.

He strides up, offering his hand. HOWARD forces himself to take BREWSTER's hand and shake firmly.

								HOWARD
Owen, nice to see you again.

								BREWSTER
(to MAID)
Emma, you can set up lunch now . . . *(he ushers HOWARD into the living room)* . . . Come on in.

								HOWARD
Really lovely room . . . *(checks the panoramic view from the window)* . . . View, too. That's nice.

								BREWSTER
Sit down . . . *(HOWARD sits on the sofa)* . . . Thanks for coming by. Just thought you and I should have a chance to talk privately. Away from the office.

								HOWARD
I appreciate that, Owen.

A beat.

								BREWSTER
So . . . you're coming out pretty strong against the C.A.B. bill.

								HOWARD
You're coming on pretty strong for it.

BREWSTER

It's my bill, Howard, I sincerely believe America cannot afford more than one international carrier.

HOWARD

You think it's fair for one airline to have a monopoly on international travel?

BREWSTER

I think one airline can do it better without competition. All I'm thinking about is the needs of the American passenger.

HOWARD's eye is drawn to a painting on a wall. A llama in a Peruvian setting.

HOWARD

Now that's just beautiful. What is that, a yak? Some kinda yak?

BREWSTER

A llama. The wife picked it up when we were in Peru last year.

HOWARD

A llama, sonofagun, a real llama. In Peru?

BREWSTER

Yeah, last year.

BREWSTER doesn't like the way the conversation is getting off-point. Thankfully, the **MAID** enters:

MAID

Lunch is served, Senator.

BREWSTER

(*standing*)
Come on, let's have some lunch.

He leads **HOWARD** into the dining room as:

HOWARD
Did you actually see any llamas?

BREWSTER
No, my wife just liked the painting.

HOWARD
Hell of an interesting animal. Gotta read up on those. How do you spell it? Like Fernando Lamas?

BREWSTER ushers him into the dining room. Points him to a chair:

BREWSTER
No, no, the *animal*. It has two l's. Sit down, please . . .

Their lunch plates are covered with metal domes. The **MAID** pulls them away. **BREWSTER** watches for **HOWARD**'s reaction.

The plates are filled with Brook Trout and heaps of asparagus and Brussel sprouts. The trout is served with the head on. A glassy eye stares up at **HOWARD**.

BREWSTER
It's Brook Trout. Hope you like fish.

HOWARD
Love it, thanks.

BREWSTER is disappointed. **HOWARD** forces himself to dig in. The **MAID** pours water into their glasses. **HOWARD** has the glass **BREWSTER** smudged with his thumb print before.

BREWSTER
I know you're not a drinking man, so I hope water is fine.

HOWARD sees the thumb print. Takes the glass and drinks.

HOWARD

Thanks.

BREWSTER is disappointed that his childish game of psychological warfare is failing so miserably.

BREWSTER

All right, let's talk turkey... My investigators have turned up a lot of dirt. It could be really embarrassing if this stuff got out. I'd like to save you that embarrassment.

HOWARD

That's very kind of you, Owen.

BREWSTER

My Committee has the power to hold public hearings. I'd like to spare you that.

HOWARD

Would you now?

HOWARD's sang froid is rather angering **BREWSTER**. A beat.

BREWSTER

You wanna go down in history as a war profiteer, Howard?

HOWARD stops eating. Looks at him.

HOWARD

What do you want?

BREWSTER

Agree to support my C.A.B. bill and I won't hold public hearings.

HOWARD
I can't do that, Owen. The C.A.B. would kill TWA.

BREWSTER
Sell TWA to Pan Am. You'll get a fair price.

At last. The deal.

HOWARD resumes eating, not looking at **BREWSTER**.

HOWARD
And then you won't go public?

BREWSTER
That's right. The investigation is closed and no one knows a thing. Better for everyone.

HOWARD
You know I'm still wondering one thing . . .

BREWSTER
What's that?

HOWARD
That picture of the llama you got last year. Where'd you sail from?

BREWSTER
We didn't. We flew.

HOWARD
Oh.

BREWSTER stares at him. **HOWARD** returns the stare evenly. Then, his voice low and cold:

HOWARD
You sure you wanna do this, Owen? You wanna go to war with me?

BREWSTER
It's not me, Howard—it's the United States government.

HOWARD stands.

HOWARD
Listen, tell Juan Trippe something for me . . . Thank you for the flowers. And he can kiss both sides of my ass.

He goes. **BREWSTER** glowers.

INT. MAYFLOWER HOTEL—CORRIDOR. DAY.

HOWARD moves down the corridor, away from **BREWSTER**'s apartment. He rounds a corner, where he has left his cane, and almost instantly deflates.

He leans against a wall, shaking dangerously, panting for breath. The effort of appearing "normal" for **BREWSTER** has totally exhausted him.

He can't control the tremors in his body. He finally implodes—sinking down the wall.

EXT. SENATE STEPS. DAY.

BREWSTER is giving a press conference. Assembled reporters take down every word.

BREWSTER
. . . defrauded this government of 60 million dollars while we were at war, when this country could least afford it. While brave men were dying on the beaches of Normandy, Mr. Hughes was picking the pocket of the American taxpayer.

                             REPORTER
Will Mr. Hughes be subpoenaed to appear before the
Committee?

                             BREWSTER
I'll have him dragged to Washington if I have to. I want to see
the whites of his lies. He's got some questions to answer, son.
About that monstrous boondoggle of his. That model airplane
kit. That flying lumberyard. That . . . Spruce Goose!

Flashbulbs explode as we hear **HOWARD**'s voice, whispering:

                             HOWARD (V.O.)
Someone tell me where I sleep . . .

Taking us to . . . .

INT. 7000 ROMAINE—SCREENING ROOM. DAY.

Stark desert landscapes. Clouds. Black and white.

Location footage from THE OUTLAW is being projected on the screen, the flickering light the only illumination.

                             HOWARD (V.O.)
Someone tell me where I sleep . . .

And we see him. He removes his shirt as he speaks and ranges around the screening room.

                             HOWARD
. . . I-sleep-in-this-room/In-the-dark-in-this-room/I-have-a-place-that-I-sleep/Someone-tell-me-where-I-sleep/Will-some-one-*please*-just-tell-me . . .

He drops his shirt as he wanders, more slowly now, like a windup toy running down. He notes the desert scenery being projected.

HOWARD
... I-like-the-desert/Hot-there-in-the-desert/But-clean/Good clouds ... Real fine ... clouds ... Jesus ... I need to ... Will someone ... please ...

The windup toy is done. **HOWARD** just stands there. Frozen.

HOWARD
I need to sleep ... No. No. No ... I should drink something first.

He stands looking at a neat collection of milk bottles across the room. He mimes the action with his hands slowly as he describes it. He is unaware that his hands are moving.

HOWARD
I'll walk over there and pick up a bottle of milk with my ... right hand ... and I'll take off the top with my ... left hand ... with two fingers ... of my left hand ... I'll take off the top and put it in my pocket ... my left pocket ...

His hands stop moving. He looks at the bottles of milk. He does not move.

HOWARD
How long has it been here? It might be bad ... (he begins miming the action again, with exactly the same gestures he used a moment before) ... So if the milk is bad I shouldn't walk over there ... and pick up the bottle of milk with my ... right hand ... and take off the top with my ... left hand ...

His mental loop is broken when the red light above the screening room door begins to flash. Someone is outside.

He goes to the door. He talks through the door, waging a terrible battle to sound sane.

                        HOWARD
Who is it?

Split-screen to:

KATE HEPBURN, outside the screening room.

                        KATE
Howard, it's Kate. I need to see you.

HOWARD moans. Presses his hands against the screening room door.

                        KATE
Howard, do you hear me? I'm coming in.

She tries to open the door. It is locked.

                        KATE
Unlock this door immediately.

                        HOWARD
I can't.

                        KATE
Did you say something?

                        HOWARD
(tormented)
I can't.

A beat.

                        KATE
You mean you won't.

HOWARD is dissolving, wanting more than anything in life to see her, touch her, hold her.

She is deeply concerned. Leans against the door.

KATE

(softly)
Howard . . . please let me see you.

HOWARD

I haven't shaved.

KATE

I don't care. Let me in.

HOWARD

I can hear you . . . I could always hear you. Even in the cockpit, with the engines . . .

KATE

That's because I'm so goddamn loud.

He smiles. Tears coming to his eyes. He leans his whole body against the door, wanting to be closer.

KATE

Howard, I came to thank you . . . I found out what you did for Spence and me. Buying those awful pictures.

HOWARD

You love him.

KATE

He's everything I have.

HOWARD

I'm glad for you, Kate . . . Katie.

HOWARD proceeds with great difficulty:

                         HOWARD
Go away now. Would you do that?

                          KATE
(tears)
Howard . . .

                         HOWARD
Go away, just for now, I'll see you soon. We'll go flying.

                          KATE
Please take me flying again . . . I can take the wheel . . . Howard? . . . Are you there? . . . Are you there, Howard?

A pause and then she turns and walks down the long corridor, devastated. He hears her footsteps echoing away . . .

On her half of the split-screen we see her walking away as . . .

HOWARD sinks to the floor. He holds his knees and rocks like a feral child. Inarticulate moans coming from deep within him . . .

She disappears around a corner, the hallway is empty. **HOWARD** is alone.

End split-screen.

And **HOWARD**'s journey into hell begins.

He never leaves the screening room. For months.

INT. SCREENING ROOM SEQUENCE. DAY/NIGHT

A line of ants creeps across a plate of cookies.

We don't see **HOWARD**. We see his hands.

He carefully removes a Kleenex from a box. And then another. And then another. And then a handful. He methodically wraps his hand in a wad of Kleenex to press the RECORD button on a tape recorder.

We watch the tape in the machine begin to spin.

Then we explore **HOWARD**'s strange realm—slowly coming to realize the depths of his descent . . .

                        HOWARD (V.O.)
Memo to All Staff . . . There has been some confusion on the topic of my lunch. I will clarify. The employee delivering my lunch is to use no less than four Kleenex brand tissues to carry the bag into the screening room. He is to open the bag with his right hand and then hold the bag out to me at a forty five degree angle so I may reach into the bag without touching the paper . . .

We see engine parts scattered about like corpses after a battle. We see brown paper bags and newspapers are stacked messily all around. We see grainy surveillance photos of **AVA** out on dates with other men . . .

                        HOWARD (V.O.)
. . . You must understand this is the most important thing in my life. When the milk bottles are delivered to the screening room, the employee with the bottles must wear a white shirt and no jacket. His cuffs must be completely buttoned and he must not wear a watch or jewelry or cologne of any kind . . .

We see mountains of discarded Kleenex. And boxes of Kleenex stacked in strange, geometric patterns. We see hundreds and hundreds of starlet headshots, haphazardly piled in chairs . . .

We see reels of movie film, some unspooled, the film stretching around the room like celluloid tendons. We see his clothes, discarded . . .

                    HOWARD (V.O.)
> ... The employee with the milk bottles must press the door button *seven times exactly*. When he has heard me repeat the words "Come in with the milk" ten times, with no variation, "Come in with the milk," ten times, he must then use his left hand to open the door and enter. He must not look at me ...

We return to the ants, slowly creeping across the plate of cookies. Tenacious. Omnivorous. Unstoppable.

And we finally see **HOWARD**.

He stands, naked.

He stands in front of the screen. Silent images from HELL'S ANGELS are being projected. A dogfighting scene. The planes twist and soar over his naked body.

The only sane order in this hellish place seems to be a neat row of empty milk bottles against one wall.

HOWARD slowly backs away from the screen. His whole psyche concentrating on a series of sounds ... syllables ... letters ... fighting to find order in chaos. It is *painfully emotional*. Every correct letter is a huge victory, every incorrect letter is a crushing defeat.

                    HOWARD
> Q ... U ... A ... R ...

He slowly walks to the pristine row of empty milk bottles.

                    HOWARD
> Q ... U ... A ...

He picks one up. Pees in it.

                        HOWARD
    ...R...A-E-A...N...

He finishes peeing. Carefully carries the bottle across the room to the opposite wall.

                        HOWARD
    ...Q...U...E...R...

He sets the milk bottle down. We realize there is an endless line of milk bottles on this side of the room. All filled with urine. Precisely ordered.

He looks at them. Trying not to weep. Concentrating intensely.

                        HOWARD
    ...A...R...N...T...E...E...I...N...

Then a red light reflects off the milk bottles. The door light. He goes to the door, talks through it.

                        HOWARD
Hello...?

Split-screen to:

A rather mystified **JUAN TRIPPE** outside the screening room door. A chair has been placed in the hallway. **NOAH** waits down the hall.

                        TRIPPE
Howard, it's Juan.

                        HOWARD
Oh, Juan, right, right. We had an appointment, I remember that—Listen I got a hell of a cold here. Why don't you sit down out there? Don't wanna get you sick. Never forgive myself if I got you sick. You don't wanna get sick—

HOWARD clamps a hand over his mouth, fighting with himself.

Outside, **TRIPPE** sits.

> TRIPPE
>
> Okay, Howard, I'm sitting . . . *(he begins pulling documents from his briefcase)* . . . Now, I've brought all our accountings. Pan Am is trading at 13.66 a share. TWA is trading at 4.24. If we—

> HOWARD
>
> Come on, come on, come on, come on—we both know I'm not going to sell TWA. You couldn't afford her anyway. Our domestic routes alone are worth more than twice Pan Am.

> TRIPPE
>
> Considering our stock is valued at three times yours, I find that a dubious claim, Howard.

HOWARD forces himself to concentrate, eyes shut.

> HOWARD
>
> I mean you have no domestic routes. You get TWA and you span the globe—I'm not gonna sell, and you know I'm not going to sell—Here's the point: Owen Brewster works for you.

Outside, **TRIPPE** prepares his pipe.

> TRIPPE
>
> I didn't elect Senator Brewster. We can thank the voters of Maine for that.

> HOWARD
>
> If I appear at his hearings, it might get nasty for all of us.

                           TRIPPE

I think considerably more for you. While the good people of
America lost sons at Anzio, you produced a dirty movie and
built airplanes that don't fly.

Outside, **TRIPPE** lights his pipe.

                           HOWARD

Now that's just not fair. The XF-11 flew quite well for an hour
and forty five minutes. I wish you'd been up there with me. It
was very exciting.

HOWARD smiles gleefully. Take that, you sonofabitch. Then he notices a wisp of smoke from **TRIPPE**'s pipe coming under the door. It is noxious, lethal. **HOWARD** backs away from the door.

                           TRIPPE

Be that as it may, you still have to answer for the Spruce
Goose.

                           HOWARD
                    (calling from across the room)
It's called *the Hercules*—and it'll fly goddammit!

                           TRIPPE

I hope it does. America should know what its 13 million
bought.

                           HOWARD
                    (calling from across the room)
I won't sell TWA!

Outside, **HOWARD**'s distress is all too apparent to **TRIPPE**.

                           TRIPPE

I know . . .

He leans back, the cat with the canary. **HOWARD** cautiously moves back to the door as **TRIPPE** speaks:

TRIPPE

I'm going to get it anyway. You're going to default on your loan from Equitable when Senator Brewster destroys your reputation and you can't raise additional capital for the airline. The hearings will also show Hughes Aircraft to be mismanaged and incompetent. It will go bankrupt. But you won't be insolvent. You'll still have Toolco . . . Perhaps you'll go back to Houston and rebuild your empire. I rather hope you do. By that time Pan Am will have bought TWA and painted all those magnificent Connies blue and white. So, when you do return, it will be on a Pan Am plane.

HOWARD stands right at the door.

HOWARD

You seem to have me in a corner, buddy. Not a position in which I'm very comfortable.

TRIPPE

I think you'll be less comfortable at Senator Brewster's hearings. Very public, Howard. Lots of cameras and newsmen. I understand you're not particularly comfortable in crowds.

TRIPPE's droll understatement makes **HOWARD** smile.

TRIPPE

Perhaps we should spare you that.

HOWARD

Thanks for your concern. I find that very moving . . . It's been a real pleasure, Juan. Noah will take you back to the airport. Fly safe.

Outside, **TRIPPE** stands.

> TRIPPE
>
> Thank you, Howard. Take care of that cold.
>
> HOWARD
>
> I certainly will. Bye bye.

He thrusts his ear to the door, listening. Making sure **TRIPPE** is gone. He hears **TRIPPE** and **NOAH** moving away.

End *split-screen.*

HOWARD leans against the door, panting. The exertion of talking with **TRIPPE** has absolutely exhausted him.

Then he again moves to the HELL'S ANGELS footage on the screen. The planes twist and fly over his naked body.

INT. 7000 ROMAINE—CORRIDOR. DAY.

NOAH and **JUAN TRIPPE** head down the corridor to the elevator. A look approaching sympathy on **TRIPPE**'s face.

> TRIPPE
>
> *(quietly)*
>
> If you let him appear at the hearings the whole world will see what he's become . . . People should remember him as he was.

NOAH does not respond.

> TRIPPE
>
> He'll get a subpoena in three days to appear in Washington.

NOAH does not respond, but the pain to him of **HOWARD**'s madness is clear in his eyes.

They move away and we remain in the hallway.

Time-lapse to . . .

INT. 7000 ROMAINE—CORRIDOR. NIGHT.

The door to the screening room opens slightly. **HOWARD** peeks out. A few employees move about in the corridor.

He carefully steps from the screening room, standing in the doorway, not quite ready to leave his sanctuary. He has put on some clothes.

A **FEMALE SECRETARY** stops when she sees **HOWARD**. She is absolutely amazed, no one has actually seen **HOWARD** for months.

She is a bit frightened at his appearance.

> SECRETARY
> Mr. Hughes . . . ?

> HOWARD
> *(a whisper)*
> I don't have any shoes. Can you get me some shoes?

INT. MUIRFIELD. NIGHT.

HOWARD sits on the floor in his den, wearing only an old bathrobe. He is unshaven, his eyes red with exhaustion and spent tears.

He aimlessly sorts through a mountain of legal documents, trying to prepare himself for his upcoming appearance in Washington.

The doorbell rings. He pulls himself up and slowly moves through the silent house. He is fragile, moving unsteadily. He is a man made of straw, as if a wisp of air could blow him away.

He looks through the peephole and then pulls a wad of Kleenex from a waiting box. He uses the Kleenex to open the front door.

It is **AVA**. She looks at him, stunned. Recovers quickly.

AVA

How nice of you to dress for me . . . Can I come in?

HOWARD

You can come in.

He nervously looks past her as she enters. He shuts the door behind her and locks it with ritualistic precision.

HOWARD

Thanks for coming.

AVA

(offers him her wrap)
Wanna hang this up?

He looks at her wrap. Doesn't move.

AVA

Hang this up for me, Howard . . . Go on, take it.

He quickly grabs a new wad of Kleenex and uses it to take her stole and quickly hang it up in a hall closet.

AVA

Now let's get a drink . . .

HOWARD

No, wait, wait, wait—you can't move—you're safe here. You're in the germ free zone now, you understand?

AVA notes this area of the entry hall is marked off by a web of electrical tape.

              AVA
I'll take my chances.

She pushes through the tape and moves into the house.

              HOWARD
No, no, honey, please . . .

HOWARD follows nervously as she strides through the airless, darkened house to the living room. She notes all the windows are taped shut with the black electrical tape and strange webs of cascading tape criss-cross the room in mad patterns.

She also cannot help noticing the mountains of Kleenex discarded everywhere on the floor.

              AVA
Love what you've done with the place . . . (she pours herself a drink) . . . Kleenex carpet's a cute idea. Now let me look at you.

She switches on a table lamp. He stands before her. Holding his robe closed tightly.

              AVA
Drop the robe.

He removes the robe. He stands naked. She gazes over him.

              AVA
Okay, you need to eat for one . . . and a shower might be in order . . . (*her eyes play over him a bit more, mischievous*) . . . Well, I always said they don't call it Hughes Tool for nothing.

He actually smiles.

INT. MUIRFIELD-MASTER BATHROOM. NIGHT.

He stands. She shaves him.

AVA
When do you go to Washington?

HOWARD
A week. No, just under a week. I don't know the date today. But I have to be . . . I have to be . . .

AVA
All right, take it easy.

A silent beat as she shaves him. His eyes are drawn to the sink, the running water, the soap.

HOWARD'S POV—EXTREME CLOSEUP—the gleaming white porcelain sink, the tap water rinsing off the shining razor, the tiny beard hairs swirling down the drain—

AVA
There's nothing there, Howard.

A silent pause as she shaves him.

HOWARD
I see things.

AVA
I know, baby. Rinse your face off now.

She steps aside. He faces the sink. Slowly reaches forward. Stops.

AVA
Put your hands in the water and wash off the soap. I'm right here. I'm not going anywhere.

				HOWARD

Does it look clean to you?

				AVA

Nothing's clean, Howard. But we do our best, right?

He slowly reaches forward and puts his hands into the running water. He carefully washes the soap off his face. A triumph. He looks at her.

				AVA

Great. Now I want you in the shower.

				HOWARD

Don't go anywhere.

				AVA

Hell, I'd soap you up myself but I know how frisky you get.

He smiles and steps toward the shower.

EXT. MUIRFIELD—MASTER SUITE. DAY.

HOWARD stands unsteadily before a mirror, as presentable as **AVA** can make him. Clean, hair slicked down, nails cut, new suit.

				AVA

What do you think?

				HOWARD

I look all right . . .

				AVA

You look great.

				HOWARD

Will you marry me?

                              AVA
    You're too crazy for me.

She looks at him tenderly in the mirror.

                              AVA
    I gotta go, baby.

                            HOWARD
    Okay . . . Thanks.

She kisses him gently.

                              AVA
    You'd do it for me.

He nods. She goes. He stands for a moment, looking at himself in the mirror. Cosmetically at least, he has improved. But his eyes still reflect the chaos inside him.

INT. SENATE CAUCUS ROOM. DAY.

Barely controlled hysteria.

The Senate Caucus Room is jammed. 1,500 spectators and reporters are packed into a chamber built to handle 600. Hundreds more crowd the hallway outside.

Title: August 6, 1947. Brewster Senate Hearings. Day One.

The witness table holds a cluster of microphones from seven radio stations. Six newsreel cameras purr alongside an amazing new invention: a television camera. This was the first congressional hearing in history to be televised live.

Across from the witness table, **OWEN BREWSTER** sits at a long dais with the rest of his committee.

Then a sound, growing from outside the chamber, a building rumble of excited voices. **BREWSTER** glances up from his notes to see **HOWARD** walking into the chamber with **NOAH**. **HOWARD** wears a crisp new grey suit.

The photographers snap photos, a barrage of flashbulbs, an excited clamor from the spectators.

HOWARD ignores the press and spectators and goes to the witness table. Sits. **NOAH** sits next to him, begins unloading two heavy briefcases full of documents.

Then *blinding* lights suddenly snap on, focused on **HOWARD**. They are the lights to assist the new TV camera. The lights are so powerful that many of the reporters put on sunglasses. It is a surreal image as the reporters don the sunglasses and the cold eye of the TV camera gazes at **HOWARD**.

HOWARD looks almost robotic, flattened, unfocused.

BREWSTER knows he is going to slaughter him. He bangs a gavel for order.

> BREWSTER
> The committee will come to order. Mr. Hughes, will you raise your right hand and be sworn?

HOWARD stands, raises his right hand. Another barrage of flashbulbs. **HOWARD**'s pupil's dilate and undilate furiously in the strobe-like flashes.

> BREWSTER
> Do you solemnly swear that in the matter now pending before this committee, you will tell the truth, the whole truth, and nothing but the truth, so help you God?

> HOWARD
> I do.

He sits.

BREWSTER

Mr. Hughes, it is the intention of this committee—

NOAH

Mr. Hughes has a statement.

BREWSTER

Very well. Mr. Hughes, you may proceed.

NOAH holds out a piece of paper to **HOWARD**. **HOWARD** glances at it. Glances away. He says nothing.

An awkward beat.

BREWSTER

Mr. Hughes? You may proceed . . .

NOAH is getting nervous. He offers the statement to **HOWARD** again. **HOWARD** won't take it. Then **HOWARD** looks off to the press, who stare back at him. At the cruel eye of the TV camera. Then **HOWARD** looks back to **BREWSTER**.

And his eyes begin to flicker with something we've seen before. **HOWARD** ignores the prepared statement.

HOWARD

You know, I'm gonna attempt to be, um, honest here . . .

A beat. **NOAH** is terrified of what **HOWARD** is going to say. **HOWARD** focuses, glaring at **BREWSTER**.

HOWARD

Senator Brewster, if you hadn't gone too far overboard, I might have been willing to take a certain shellacking in this publicity spree of yours. I might have been willing to sit back and take a certain amount of abuse simply because I am only a private citizen while you are a Senator with all sorts of powers—But I think this goddamn circus has gone on long enough—

BREWSTER bangs his gavel—

BREWSTER
That's quite sufficient, Mr. Hughes—

HOWARD
(*angry*)
You have called me a liar, sir. In the press. You have called me a liar and a thief and a war profiteer—

BREWSTER
(*banging gavel*)
The witness will restrain his comments and—

HOWARD stands, a stunningly simple act that silences **BREWSTER** and rivets the entire room. He leans forward on the table, speaking with clipped, barely controlled anger:

HOWARD
Why not tell the truth for once, Senator? Why not tell that this investigation was really born on the day that TWA first decided to fly to Europe? On the day when TWA first invaded Juan Trippe's territory. On the day when TWA first challenged the generally accepted theory that only Juan Trippe's great Pan American Airways had the sacred right to fly the Atlantic!

The bombshell explodes. The spectators love seeing **HOWARD**, still America's Aviation Hero, defending himself. The photographers flash pictures. **BREWSTER** bangs his gavel to no avail.

HOWARD continues to stand.

We sweep across the approving spectators and then sweep back to the next day . . .

HOWARD is sitting, leaning an elbow on the table, holding an amplifier earpiece to his ear to hear BREWSTER. Completely focused.

Title: Day Two.

BREWSTER
. . . have in our possession receipts in the amount of 170,000 dollars from Mr. John Meyer. Mr. Meyer works for you, does he not?

HOWARD
He does.

BREWSTER
And what is his official title?

HOWARD
I don't exactly know. A lot of people work for me.

A chuckle from the crowd.

BREWSTER
Can you describe his duties?

HOWARD
He's sort of a press agent.

BREWSTER
Thank you, Mr. Hughes. Can you tell me why your press agent paid out more than 170,000 dollars to representatives of the United States Air Force?

HOWARD

I suppose you'd have to ask him.

BREWSTER

Can you produce him?

HOWARD

Produce him?

BREWSTER

Will you cause him to appear?

HOWARD

Senator, you had Mr. Meyer on the stand for three days last week.

BREWSTER

Be that as it may, will you ask him to return?

HOWARD

No, Senator, I don't think I will.

BREWSTER

Well, will you *try* to have him return?

HOWARD

No, Senator, I don't think I'll try.

BREWSTER

You don't think you'll try?

HOWARD

No, I don't think so.

The spectators are amused. **BREWSTER** raps his gavel quickly. Regains his composure.

BREWSTER
Mr. Hughes, the 170,000 dollars paid out to delegates of the Air Force in the form of hotel suites, TWA stock . . . female companionship . . . might these be considered bribes?

HOWARD
Yes, I suppose they could be.

BREWSTER is floored.

BREWSTER
Would you repeat that?

HOWARD
Yes, I suppose you could consider them bribes.

BREWSTER
(can't believe his luck)
Well, would you care to explain that, Mr. Hughes?

HOWARD
I'm afraid you don't know how the aviation business works, Senator. Wining and dining Air Force dignitaries is common in our business, because we all want the contracts. All the big aircraft companies do it. Now I don't know whether it's a good system or not. I just know it's not illegal. You, Senator, are the lawmaker, if you pass a law that no one can entertain Air Force officials, hell, I'll be glad to abide by it.

HOWARD leans back. **BREWSTER** is stunned. **HOWARD** has just deflated the issue through his absolute candor. The crowd loves seeing the pompous Senator taken down a few pegs.

We sweep over the impressed crowd and sweep back to the next day . . .

HOWARD is angry, leaning forward. The witness has become the inquisitor.

Title: Day Three.

                            HOWARD

...and on February 12th of this year, in your suite at the Mayflower Hotel, did you or did you not tell me that if I would sell TWA to Pan Am this investigation would be called off?

                            BREWSTER

(shrill)
I did not.

                            HOWARD

How long have you known Juan Trippe?

                            BREWSTER

I have known Mr. Trippe for several years. But—

NOAH slides **HOWARD** a piece of paper, he doesn't need to look at it.

                            HOWARD

Is it not true, Senator Brewster, that Juan Trippe donated 20,000 dollars to your last campaign and—?

                            BREWSTER

I have a personal friendship with Mr. Trippe that is—um—divorced from my duties as a Senator.

                            HOWARD

Is it not true that you accept free tickets from Pan Am so you can circle the globe in support of your C.A.B. bill?

                            BREWSTER

It is not.

                            HOWARD

Who wrote that bill, Senator?

BREWSTER

I don't understand the purpose of—

HOWARD

Who actually wrote the C.A.B. bill? The actual words in the bill. Did you write them, Senator?

BREWSTER

Mr. Hughes, this is—

HOWARD

I have it here, maybe that will refresh your memory... (**NOAH** *hands him a copy of the bill*)... Here we go. Bill S. 987 to amend the Civil Aeronautics Act. You introduced this bill into the Senate. Lotta words. You write all of them?

BREWSTER sputters.

HOWARD

You write *any* of them?

BREWSTER

Now see here, Mr. Hughes—

HOWARD

This entire bill was written by *Pan Am executives* and designed to give that airline a *monopoly* on international travel! And you've been flogging this bill on their behalf all around the world, have you not?!

BREWSTER

My duties take me to—

HOWARD

What in hell does a Senator from Maine need to visit Peru for?

BREWSTER
(*flustered*)
I was—ah—seeking outlets for our trade goods.

HOWARD
They buy a lot of lobsters down there, do they?

BREWSTER
I—

HOWARD
How many times have you been to Mr. Trippe's office in New York in the last three months? . . . (**BREWSTER** *stops cold*) . . . Would you like me to tell you, Senator?

BREWSTER
(*exploding*)
This has gone on long enough—Juan Trippe is a great American and his airline has advanced the cause of commercial aviation in this country for decades! Juan Trippe is a patriot! Juan Trippe isn't a man interested in making money!

HOWARD lets **BREWSTER**'s absurd final words echo around the chamber. He leans back.

HOWARD
Well, I'm sure his stockholders will be happy to hear that.

Chuckles from the spectators.

We sweep over the spectators and sweep back to the next day . . .

HOWARD is leaning back, holding the amplifier earpiece to his ear. **NOAH** is exhausted, the days of grueling testimony taking a toll. **HOWARD** is completely on top of his game.

The chamber is silent, the reporters and spectators straining to catch every word. This is really it.

Title: Day Four.

BREWSTER

Did you receive 43 million dollars to manufacture 100 XF-11 spy planes for the United States Air Force?

HOWARD

I did.

BREWSTER

How many functional planes were delivered to the United States Air Force?

HOWARD

None.

BREWSTER

Would you lean a little closer to the microphones, sir?

HOWARD

(leaning in)
None.

BREWSTER

Did you receive 13 million dollars from the United States Air Force to manufacture a prototype flying boat, known as The Hercules?

HOWARD

I did.

BREWSTER

Did you deliver that plane?

HOWARD
I did not.

BREWSTER
So, by your admission in this chamber you received 56 million dollars from the United States government for planes you did not deliver.

HOWARD
That is correct.

BREWSTER thinks he has him. But can't help pushing the dagger in a bit.

BREWSTER
Well, excuse me for asking, Mr. Hughes, but where did all that money go?

HOWARD
It went into the planes. And a lot more.

BREWSTER
(leans back, satisfied)
More? . . . Do tell, Mr. Hughes, what other larcenies have you committed?

HOWARD
I mean my money, sir.

BREWSTER is immediately alarmed, realizes he has stumbled badly. He has given **HOWARD** the opening he has been waiting for.

BREWSTER
Mr. Hughes, your personal finances are not the—

ANOTHER SENATOR
Let him speak.

BREWSTER glances at the other Senators. They stare back at him coldly.
BREWSTER sees the waiting press and spectators.

BREWSTER

Proceed, Mr. Hughes.

HOWARD

(very quietly)
You see the thing is I care very much about aviation. It's been the great joy of my life. So I put my own money into these planes . . . I've lost millions, Mr. Chairman. And I'll go on losing millions. It's just what I do.

The chamber is silent. Hanging on every word.

HOWARD

And if I lost a lot of the government's money during the war, I hope folks will put that in perspective . . . More than 60 other airplanes ordered from such firms as Boeing and Lockheed and Douglas and Northrop never saw action either. In all, more than 800 million dollars was spent during the war on planes that never flew. More than 6 *billion* on other weapons that were never delivered.

A beat. The coup de grace:

HOWARD

And yet Hughes Aircraft—with her 56 million—is the only firm under investigation here today.

A tremor through the chamber.

HOWARD

I can't help but think that has a little more to do with TWA than with planes that didn't fly.

BREWSTER slumps.

> HOWARD
>
> I have only one more thing to say to this committee, and that's about the Hercules... Now, I'm supposed to be many things which are not complimentary. I am supposed to be capricious. I have been called a playboy. I have even been called an eccentric. But I do not believe I have the reputation of being a liar... I put the sweat of my life into this thing. My reputation is wrapped up in it. So believe me when I say that if the Hercules fails to fly, I will leave the country and I will not return. And I mean it.

Then **HOWARD** stands.

> HOWARD
>
> Now Mr. Chairman... you can subpoena me, you can arrest me, you can claim I've taken a run-out powder, but I've had enough of this nonsense. Good afternoon.

He turns and begins walking out. The spectators heartily approve. A smattering of applause.

BREWSTER sinks in his chair. It's over. **HOWARD** has won.

HOWARD continues to walk out of the chamber as the crowd applauds.

This image is exactly mirrored in...

INT. JUAN TRIPPE'S OFFICE—PAN AM. DAY.

...the tiny black-and-white screen of **JUAN TRIPPE**'s new television set.

TRIPPE sits with a number of his **EXECUTIVES**.

TRIPPE sighs.

                    TRIPPE

Switch it off.

                    EXECUTIVE

But the hearings aren't—

                    TRIPPE

The hearings are over.

An **EXECUTIVE** turns off the TV.

Silence as **TRIPPE** slowly rises and wanders to his massive globe. He stares at the globe for a moment, clearly seeing the future.

                    TRIPPE

The C.A.B. bill will be defeated in the Senate. TWA will begin flights from New York to Paris. And then on to Moscow to Japan to Hawaii to Los Angeles to New York.

He continues to look at the globe. The world. His world. Not anymore. **HOWARD**'s world.

                    TRIPPE

Fuck.

EXT. LONG BEACH HARBOR. DAY.

Like a great white leviathan, the Hercules bobs in the water far out in Long Beach Harbor. It is absurd. It is grandiose. It is magnificent.

Title: November 2, 1947

And the harbor is jammed. Scores of reporters and thousands of spectators fill every inch along the piers. Hundreds of boats cruise the harbor. Planes circle overhead. Newsreel cameras film.

INT./EXT. HERCULES. DAY.

HOWARD, GLENN and **PROFESSOR FITZ** climb the stairs to the flight deck.

It is gleaming, busy and elegant. And, of course, huge.

A dozen engineers, technicians, navigators and radio operators are already at their complex instrument panels. **PROFESSOR FITZ** gazes around at everything.

> HOWARD
> Come up front, Professor . . .

PROFESSOR FITZ walks with **HOWARD** and **GLENN** to the forward stations. **GLENN** straps himself into the co-pilot's seat, switches on his units.

HOWARD settles into the pilot's seat as **PROFESSOR FITZ** nervously glances out one of the forward windows. The choppy waves of the harbor are very far below.

> HOWARD
> Why don't you strap yourself in right over there—(points to an auxiliary engineer's station)—should be able to see great.

PROFESSOR FITZ does so, struggling a bit with the restraint harness.

HOWARD makes a quick visual check of the complex instrument panel before him. It is a beautiful anarchy of dials, instruments and gauges. A series of four throttle levers to his right and an elegantly designed wheel ahead of him.

He finally touches the sacred wheel. It feels right.

> HOWARD
> Okay, Odie, let's power her up.

Outside:

We see **HOWARD** through the front windows of the Hercules, flipping various switches. Then we pull back . . . and back . . . **HOWARD** growing smaller . . . and smaller . . .

Finally his face is a tiny speck in the forward window of the mammoth plane . . .

As the plane's eight propellers slowly begin to spin.

Inside:

An echoing, distant thrum from the massive props.

> **HOWARD**
> Advancing master throttles.

> **GLENN**
> Advancing master throttles.

HOWARD reaches to his side and gently pushes the four large throttle levers forward with his right hand as his left hand controls the wheel.

Outside:

The Hercules begins to move. Cheers from the thousands of spectators on shore.

Inside:

> **GLENN**
> Veniers are in sequence.

> **HOWARD**
> Understood. Lower fifteen degrees of flaps.

GLENN
Lowering fifteen degrees of flaps . . . *(he glances to* **HOWARD***)*
. . . She's gotta hit 70 mph to have a chance.

HOWARD gently plays the throttle levers, his fingers undulating like a pianist's, feeling them respond.

Outside:

The Hercules picks up speed. Splashing through the waves.

Inside:

HOWARD gently plays the throttles, enjoying the feel of the plane.

GLENN
25 mph . . . 30 . . . 35—take it easy, Howard—40 mph.

The flight deck is rocking and bouncing now in the choppy waves.

PROFESSOR FITZ holds on tightly.

Outside:

The Hercules picks up speed, crashing over the waves.

Inside:

The whole flight deck is jumping and vibrating now as the plane crashes through the waves.

HOWARD
Throttling back for starboard turn 1-8-0.

GLENN
Throttling back for starboard turn 1-8-0.

HOWARD slows the plane, gently turning her. A perfect turn, the great beast responding to his delicate touch on the controls.

HOWARD slows to a stop. The plane waits. The engines rumble obediently.

> HOWARD
>
> How does she sound, Odie?

> GLENN
>
> Sounds good.

> HOWARD
>
> *(to* **FITZ***)*
>
> Professor, would you do me a favor? Would you look out that window there and tell me what the wind's doing?

PROFESSOR FITZ peers out the window, trying to gauge the wind. His eyes dart from the waves below to a bird flying above, anything to give him a sense of speed and direction.

> PROFESSOR FITZ
>
> I would say we have a . . . 15 knot wind.

> HOWARD
>
> Would you call that a tailwind, Professor?

> PROFESSOR FITZ
>
> I would, Mr. Hughes.

HOWARD glances to **GLENN**. Pokes his lucky fedora a little higher on his head.

> HOWARD
>
> Advancing master throttles.

                        GLENN
    Advancing master throttles.

HOWARD gently folds his fingers around the throttles and applies pressure. The Hercules begins to move forward.

Picking up speed—

Outside:

The Hercules crashes through the waves—

Inside:

HOWARD forces the throttle levers a bit more, still gently controlling the wheel with his left hand.

                        HOWARD
    Lemme hear it, Odie.

                        GLENN
    25 mph . . . 30 . . . 35 . . . 40 . . .

Outside:

The Hercules is racing through the waves now—

Inside:

                        GLENN
    . . . 45 . . . 50 . . . 55 . . .

The roar of the engines and vibrations of the plane echo through the wooden ship bizarrely. The wood creaking and moaning—

Outside:

The Hercules is zooming through the water, sending up great sprays of white foam—

Inside:

The roar is deafening. The whole ship is bouncing and shaking violently. The throttles vibrate slightly under **HOWARD**'s firm right hand. His left hand is still gentle on the wheel. In complete control. His eyes totally focused ahead.

                       GLENN
...60...65...70...75!

Now.

HOWARD gives a final caress to the throttles and—

Outside:

The Hercules leaves the water.

Inside:

The terrible bouncing and vibrations abruptly stop. Silence but for the roar of the engines.

A stunned moment of realization.

The Hercules is airborne.

Outside:

The Hercules flies.

Inside:

The whole flight deck is roaring with cheers and laughter.

Outside:

The Hercules. The Spruce Goose. **HOWARD**'s Pet Monster.

Soars.

INT. HANGAR—LONG BEACH. DAY.

The mighty Hercules is back in her berth.

She overlooks a celebration party. Mobs of friends and well-wishers. **JOHNNY MEYER** is talking with **AVA**. **JACK FRYE** is conferring happily with TWA executives.

HOWARD stands with an arm around **PROFESSOR FITZ**, shaking hands and reliving the flight.

> HOWARD
> ... Hell, I don't deserve the credit. All goes to Professor Fitz here, he made the wind blow right. Couldn't have done it without him ... Excuse me.

HOWARD sees **AVA** and **JOHNNY MEYER** across the room. Goes to them and snatches **AVA** away:

> HOWARD
> Excuse us, Johnny ... *(he walks with her)* ... Feel like going to Paris?

> AVA
> Now?

> HOWARD
> Couple months. TWA's starting up flights to Europe. Thought I might pilot the first one myself. Oughta be some fun.

AVA

Lots of good shopping in Paris.

HOWARD

I'll buy you anything you want.

AVA

(*stops*)
You can buy me dinner, how about that?

HOWARD

Dinner then. We got a date?

AVA

Okay, baby, you got a date.

He kisses her and then sees **NOAH** and **GLENN ODEKIRK** across the room.

HOWARD

I'll be back in a second. Don't go anywhere.

He goes to **NOAH** and **GLENN**:

HOWARD

Glad you're both here, now listen, I've been thinking about something. Something new—*jet airplanes*. You know anything about jets?

NOAH

(*wary*)
No . . . but it sounds expensive.

HOWARD

Oh, it will be. But we gotta get started. Walk with me.

They walk with **HOWARD** as he strides, strategizing—

####### HOWARD

Whoever can start utilizing jet technology on commercial airliners is gonna win all the marbles, you understand? Jets give you almost unlimited speed and range. Damn things are rocket ships! . . . Odie, what do you know about the technology?

####### GLENN

Not a lot.

HOWARD stops.

He sees a trio of **CLEAN YOUNG MEN** in clean black suits watching him from across the hangar. Their gaze is even, but in their studied neutrality there is something menacing.

####### HOWARD

Noah—who are those guys? They work for me?

####### NOAH

Everyone works for you, Howard.

HOWARD resumes walking as he continues to **GLENN**:

####### HOWARD

Now, listen, Lockheed worked on the F-80. Let's get Bob Gross on the phone and see if he can help us out.

####### GLENN

Now?

####### HOWARD

'Course now. We gotta get into it. Jets are gonna be the way of the future. The way of the future. The way of the future. The way of the future . . .

HOWARD stops.

GLENN and NOAH look at him. Not wanting to believe.

                    HOWARD
The way of the future. The way of the future. The way of the future. The way of the future . . .

HOWARD's face.

Panic. Fear.

He is defenseless.

It's finished.

                    HOWARD
The way of the future. The way of the future. The way of the future . . .

Then HOWARD sees that the CLEAN YOUNG MEN are now moving . . . heading in his direction . . . strategically moving through the party guests like assassins . . .

                    HOWARD
The way of the future. The way of the future. The way of the future. The way of the future . . .

NOAH quickly takes HOWARD's arm and begins to pull him through the party.

                    NOAH
Help me out here, Glenn . . .

GLENN helps NOAH lead HOWARD through the party.

HOWARD glances at the approaching CLEAN YOUNG MEN. While their neutral expressions do not change, their approach is predatory.

HOWARD

The way of the future. The way of the future. The way of the future . . .

NOAH and GLENN lead HOWARD to a bathroom. GLENN quickly checks the bathroom, empty. He and NOAH gently push HOWARD inside as:

NOAH

(to HOWARD)
Stay here. I'll be right back. All right?

GLENN

Do you understand, Howard?

HOWARD

(nods)
The way of the future. The way of the future . . .

NOAH

(quickly to GLENN)
Guard the door. I'll get a doctor. *No one sees him like this.*

GLENN shuts the bathroom door as NOAH hurries away.

INT. HANGAR—BATHROOM. FOLLOWING.

HOWARD stands in the filthy hangar bathroom, looking around.

HOWARD

The way of the future. The way of the future. The way of the future . . .

He goes to a filthy sink. Reaches out to wash his hands—

HOWARD'S POV—EXTREME CLOSEUP—the sink. It really is filthy this time. A foul, stained cauldron.

HOWARD stops. Hands suspended midair.

> HOWARD
> The way of the future. The way of the future. The way of the future . . .

He looks up at himself in the dingy mirror over the sink.

In his eyes, he sees it all.

His future.

Already written.

> HOWARD
> The way of the future. The way of the future. The way of the future . . .

Then . . . he sees something reflected in the mirror . . . behind him . . .

In the mirror, **HOWARD** sees . . .

YOUNG HOWARD. The same boy we met at the opening of the story. The same serious expression and deep, dark eyes.

YOUNG HOWARD stands, calmly looking at **HOWARD**.

> YOUNG HOWARD
> When I grow up . . . I want to fly the fastest planes ever built. And make the biggest movies ever. And be the richest man in the world.

A beat as **YOUNG HOWARD** continues to look at **HOWARD**.

Then he fades into darkness as **HOWARD** slowly looks back to his own face in the mirror.

HOWARD considers himself.

In his eyes we now see a strange form of acceptance. Of triumph.

Maybe even of peace.

HOWARD
The way of the future. The way of the future. The way of the future . . .

Fade to black.

The End